The Stoic idea of the city

A BEAUTIFUL DWELLING PLACE IS BUILT FOR ITS OWNERS AND NOT FOR MICE, IN THE SAME WAY WE MUST REGARD THE UNIVERSE AS THE DWELLING PLACE OF THE GODS.

The Stoic idea of the city

MALCOLM SCHOFIELD
Professor of Ancient Philosophy,
University of Cambridge

With a new Foreword by
MARTHA C. NUSSBAUM

and a new Epilogue
by the author

THE UNIVERSITY OF CHICAGO PRESS
Chicago & London

The University of Chicago Press, Chicago 60637
The University of Chicago Press, Ltd., London

08 07 06 05 04 03 02 01 00 99 1 2 3 4 5

ISBN: 0-226-74006-4 (paper)

Library of Congress Cataloging-in-Publication Data

Schofield, Malcolm.
The stoic idea of the city / Malcolm Schofield.
p. cm.
Reprint. Originally published: Cambridge, England : Cambridge University Press, 1991. With new epilogue. Includes bibliographical references and index.
ISBN 0-226-74006-4 (pbk. : alk. paper)
1. Political science—Greece—History. 2. Natural law—History. 3. Stoics—History. I. Title.
JC73.S366 1999
320'.0938—dc21 98-56196
CIP

♾ The paper used in this publication meets the minimum requirements of the American National Standard for Information Sciences—Permanence of Paper for Printed Library Materials, ANSI Z39.48-1992.

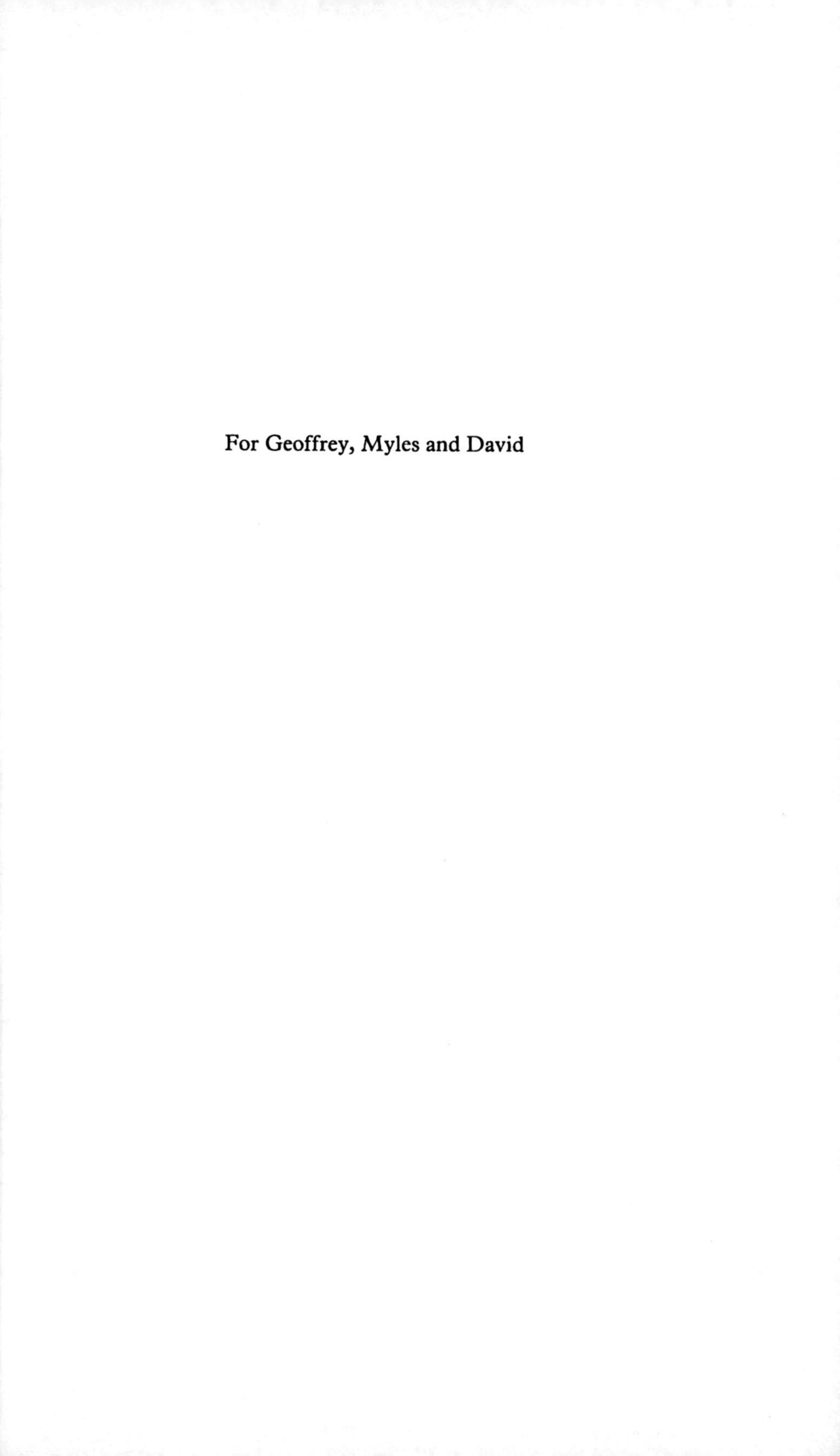

For Geoffrey, Myles and David

Contents

Foreword

Malcolm Schofield's *The Stoic Idea of the City* is a landmark in the study of ancient Greek political thought. For many years scholars and teachers in that field have focused on the ideas of Plato and Aristotle and have almost entirely neglected the important and historically influential ideas of the Stoic school. Insofar as the Stoics are considered, historians tend to focus on the copious surviving writings of Roman authors such as Cicero, Seneca, and Marcus Aurelius, rather than on the fragmentary evidence about the earlier Greek Stoics, who were the original sources of most of the ideas of these Roman authors. And yet we know that both Zeno of Citium (334–262 B.C.E.) and Chrysippus (c. 280–206 B.C.E.), the two most important philosophers of the Greek Stoa, wrote works of ideal political theory entitled *Republic*, works that in some respects followed Plato, but that also sharply departed from Plato, especially in the treatment of desire, sexuality, and the body. Chrysippus, Zeno's distinguished successor, transformed Plato's idea of a community ruled by sages into the idea of a cosmic city ruled by laws linking both gods and men.

Although the writings of Zeno and Chrysippus survive only in fragments, their distinction as philosophers is evident from the accounts that do survive. Chrysippus, in particular, was evidently one of the most creative and influential philosophers in the entire Western tradition. He invented (probably along with Zeno) both propositional logic and the philosophy of language; he wrote what seem to be some of the most interesting analyses of emotion ever produced; he wrote distinguished works on ethical choice; and he developed ideas of natural law that have been important to political thought ever since. These two philosophers had a huge influence on Roman thinkers, both Stoic and anti-Stoic, whose work we do know, and, through them, on later philosophers such as Descartes, Spinoza, Grotius, Adam Smith, Rousseau, and Kant.

Schofield's book is the first systematic attempt to set out what can be reconstructed about the Greek Stoics' original and highly influential works of political philosophy, setting them in their historical context and making sense of their prescriptions. It is very difficult to do this, because the evidence about Greek Stoic ideas is fragmentary, and is transmitted in authors who vary widely in both date and degree of reliability. It takes first-class scholarship and a judicious mind to make sense of all the evidence; and this Schofield does in a superlative way.

The most famous legacy of Stoic political thought to modernity is the idea of "natural law" and the related notion of "world citizenship." Before the Stoics, Greek political thought focused on the polis; there was no developed doctrine about obligations of respect and mutual aid to human beings dwelling outside one's own city. The Stoics, however, held that the worth of reason and moral capacity makes us all members of a single virtual city, governed by a set of binding moral norms to which actual laws are held accountable.

Schofield argues that the Greek Stoics conceived of an ideal city as a city in which distinctions of local origin, birth, class, and even sex are treated as irrelevant to citizenship and civic functioning. The only significant fact about a person, from the political point of view, is the potential for virtue, and this is a sufficient condition for citizenship in the ideal city. The ideal city thus accords citizenship equally to male and to female, eradicating conventional gender roles (there is even a provision for unisex clothing!), and uprooting the pride people standardly feel in their local group memberships. Because a city so conceived does not think of itself as bound to its own locality, a doctrine of world citizenship was closely connected to this moral ideal. The Stoics held that at a deep moral level we are all citizens of one world, bound to one another by ties of both affiliation and obligation. This did not mean that they endorsed a world state; it did mean that they saw all civic decisions as regulated by the idea of a virtual moral community of humanity in the world as a whole. In this community all citizens will be at the deepest level "citizens of the world," kosmopolitai. (It was this idea, in Greek Stoicism, that shaped the "cosmopolitan" thought of Cicero and Marcus, and, through them, later thinkers such as Grotius and Kant.)

Schofield believes that there is another less famous aspect of Stoic thought that is just as important as the cosmic city for an understanding of their project. This is their doctrine of eros as guarantor of civic harmony. The Greek Stoics followed Plato in some respects: for example, in recognizing the potential of women for citizenship and virtue. And, like Plato, they held that marriage is a dangerous institution for the city to foster, a home of jealousy and particularized affections. They proposed to eradicate it completely, substituting a communal system of child care and a view of sexual conduct as acceptable on the basis of love and mutual "persuasion." But they implicitly criticize the repression of eros and the body in Plato's ideal city. The ideal Stoic city is held together by strong erotic ties, and citizens are encouraged to form intense erotic relationships with other citizens, on the basis of virtue and the potential for virtue. All other passions are reproved in Stoicism. Stoic citizens will have neither anger nor fear, neither pride nor jealousy nor envy, neither grief nor pity. Eros alone is exempted from the critique. Although some forms of eros are criticized, a good form of eros is recognized and assiduously cultivated. The Stoics define it as "an attempt to form a friendship, inspired by the visible beauty of young people in their prime." Sexual conduct is considered an "indifferent": that is, it can be bad if performed without ethical knowledge and/or with bad intentions, but it can be fully virtuous, if performed with ethical knowledge and with good intentions. (This position is similar to the one defended by Pausanias in Plato's *Symposium.*) Thus the erotic relations of lovers in the ideal city apparently admit sexual conduct under appropriate circumstances. Holding, as they do, that the mind itself is bodily, and denying that there is any element of the person that survives death, the Stoics have no reason to share Plato's derogatory attitude to bodily existence, or to think of the body as a mere prison-house of the soul. Their larger metaphysical views thus support their ethical views about sexuality, which probably lay closer to the popular thought of their own time than did Platonic asceticism.

This aspect of Greek Stoic theory is the topic of a great deal of later discussion, which Schofield usefully reports: Cicero thinks the Stoics are indulging in special pleading when they exempt this one passion from the general critique; he believes that they should have made their critique consistent, considering eros to be among the most dangerous and debilitating of the passions. Plutarch thinks that the Stoics' moralized view of love has not really made sufficient room for what is standardly called eros. Because their moralized eros makes no room for grief or loss, for surprise or passionate upheaval, it seems to him to be only a philosophical word-game to call it eros; it lacks much of the value of the eros of everyday experience, as well as much of the danger.

Schofield elaborates the Stoic doctrine of eros in connection with a critique and elaboration of Greek homosexual customs. Stoics argue that the basis for the sexual relationship between erastes and eromenos should be character and potential, not mere physical beauty; but they also have a complex doctrine of signs that considers physical beauty to be an expression of the soul within. Thus they view the physical aspect of sexual attraction as itself moral in nature: what really arouses us is virtue itself, and in pursuing sexual conduct we are ultimately pursuing an understanding of the ultimate good. (This part of the theory again has Platonic antecedents: the *Phaedrus* is particularly relevant. But once again, the Stoics refuse to share Plato's extreme suspiciousness of the body.) They recommend relationships of long duration between pairs of lovers, arguing that when the soul is the object of the relationship it will not fade when youthful beauty fades. One of the most valuable parts of Schofield's work is his detailed historical exploration of the Stoics' views about sexual attraction and conduct. Through a valuable account of Spartan sexual customs he sets the Stoic view in its historical context, showing why it would have seemed plausible to them that erotic relationships of the sort described could be the essential bonds of political community. At the same time, he argues that the Stoics depart from the conventional Greek ranking of male-male over male-female relationships, allowing that male-female erotic relationships may also realize a high civic value.

Schofield, among the most distinguished living experts on ancient Greek political thought, writes with a precision and detail that satisfies the most specialized scholars; but what he writes is of interest to a broad audience. Historians of ancient Greek and

Roman political thought, historians of cosmopolitan ideals in later political thought, historians of sexuality, historians of international law, and people with a general interest in classical culture will find his account valuable and persuasive.

Martha C. Nussbaum

Ernst Freund Distinguished Service Professor of Law and Ethics
Department of Philosophy, Law School, and Divinity School;
Associate, Classics Department
The University of Chicago

Preface

This book owes its origins to an invitation to write on Hellenistic political thought for the projected *Cambridge History of Hellenistic Philosophy*: part of my homework, if you like, but I hope made profitable and enjoyable for scholars and students alike. My idea has been to fill a gap on the library shelves perceived by the latter and to explore some textual material underexploited by the former.

An early version of some of the main ideas in Chapters 1, 2 and 4 was presented some years ago to a meeting of the Cambridge Philological Society and provoked a vigorous response. When the paper suddenly started to expand on revision, Cambridge University Press reacted enthusiastically to the suggestion that I might offer them a short book on the Stoic idea of the city. I have benefited from comments on a draft of the whole by Myles Burnyeat and Jaap Mansfeld. Jonathan Barnes, Peter Parsons and Michael Trapp gave me help with individual chapters, and David Sedley with some of the material now in appendixes as well as with Chapters 1 and 2. Paul Cartledge, Peter Garnsey, Neil Hopkinson and John Procopé advised me on bibliographical questions. Matthew Schofield turned two instalments of my appalling handwriting into accurate word-processing between appearances on Radio Cambridgeshire and at Hills Road Sixth Form College, and Elizabeth Schofield endured alienation of the dining-room and even more mental abstraction than usual. Shady prompted the occasion of conversations about writing with Lindsey Traub on Midsummer Common. I am grateful to them all.

The book is dedicated to three friends and colleagues with whom I have been reading ancient philosophical texts every week during term for the past decade.

M. S.

Abbreviations

References to ancient authors are given in standard forms of abbreviation. Abbreviations of journal titles used in bibliographical references in the footnotes are also standard; full versions are given under the relevant items in the bibliography. In addition note the following acronyms:

FHG *Fragmenta Historicorum Graecorum*, edited by C. and T. Müller, Paris, 1848–70

KRS G.S. Kirk, J.E. Raven and M. Schofield, *The Presocratic Philosophers*, Cambridge, 1983 (second edition)

LSJ *A Greek–English Lexicon*, compiled by H.G. Liddell and R. Scott, revised by H.S. Jones (with Supplement 1968), Oxford, 1968

RE *Paulys Realencyclopädie der classischen Altertumswissenschaft*, edited by G. Wissowa, W. Kroll and K. Mittelhaus, Stuttgart, 1893–1972

SVF *Stoicorum Veterum Fragmenta*, collected by H. von Arnim, Leipzig, 1903–5

The Stoic idea of the city

Introduction

Students of the Presocratics spend a good deal of their time on what might broadly be called doxography. Since the original writings of these thinkers have perished, we have to rely for knowledge of them on what later authors tell us. Sometimes the later sources contain quotations from the Presocratics, sometimes not, but always they present early Greek philosophy in a context and from a point of view which belongs to their own time, and is inevitably the end product of much intervening writing and thinking. 'Where does he get his information from?' 'Is it reliable?' 'Why does he give us it?' These and similar questions must constantly preoccupy anyone who reads Sextus Empiricus, Diogenes Laertius, Stobaeus, Plutarch, Hippolytus, Simplicius and other writers of the Christian era with a view to finding the truth about Presocratic philosophy.

Those who work on Hellenistic philosophy by and large devote less energy to analysis of doxography, although they are often no better supplied with original writings of the thinkers they study than their colleagues in Presocratic scholarship. I shall not speculate on what might be the reasons for this. Let me rather point out some salient facts about the evidence for the subject of this book, Stoic political thought.

The first work of Stoic political philosophy, Zeno's *Republic*, was disowned by some later Stoics and vilified by non-Stoics. For information about its contents we rely on mere scraps of doxography and on reports drawn from polemical tracts or otherwise tendentious material. There is already a considerable distance between what the *Republic* appears to have taught and the political philosophy ascribed to the Stoics e.g. by Cicero in *de finibus*, before we even begin to consider other developments. Political theory is not the main focus of any surviving treatise on the main schools of Hellenistic philosophy (contrast ethics or epistemology or theology), so we have always to be searching for pertinent ideas and arguments in a variety of late authors mainly preoccupied with other things.

What is evidently called for here is precisely the sifting and reconstruction practised by exponents of Presocratic philosophy, as they size up the authors who constitute their sources. I discovered when I got to work on the Stoic material that there was a surprising amount of quite basic work still to do in this vein, notably on the texts and concepts studied in Chapters 3 and 4 below, but even on Zeno too, despite the labours of e.g. Wachsmuth, Pearson and Baldry in previous generations and Mansfeld in our own. So various kinds of doxographical detective enquiry figure prominently in these pages.

Another comparison with the Presocratics also springs to mind. What gives work on the Presocratics much of its fascination is that it is a study of origins: the very creation of natural philosophy, metaphysics, epistemology. Stoic political philosophy represents at one and the same time a death and a birth. I shall be trying to demonstrate *inter alia* how Zeno and Chrysippus created the intellectual conditions for the demise of political philosophy in the classical republican or communitarian style of Plato and Aristotle, and for the beginnings of the natural law tradition of political thought – Zeno in dialectic with Plato, and Chrysippus in exegesis of Zeno and (perhaps more surprisingly) Heraclitus.

To bring out the distinctive flavour of the writers I discuss, and to make the book serviceable for students of philosophy and the history of political thought as well as Hellenists, I have presented in translation as many passages as possible from the sources. Summary and paraphrase tend to produce just the bland homogeneous doxography which analysis aims to penetrate; and there is a world of difference between being told that evidence indicates such and such a possibility or probability, and looking at a page of a Greek author for yourself, particularly when so many of our sources are intent on entertainment no less than edification. In general reference to texts according to the numeration of von Arnim's well-indexed *Stoicorum Veterum Fragmenta* has been avoided, since my object is to drive the reader back to the works and writers he so usefully excerpted. I do not thereby mean to pretend that *SVF* has not been my constant companion.

Cassius the Sceptic

I

The longest single report on the contents of Zeno's *Republic* that we possess is not a straightforward piece of doxography, but an account of those elements in the work to which a Sceptic called Cassius objected (D.L. VII 32–4):[1]

> But there are some, including Cassius the Sceptic and his followers, who attack Zeno on many points. They say first (1), that at the beginning of the *Republic* he proves general education useless;[2] second (2), that he says that all who are not good men are personal and public enemies, slaves, estranged from each other, parents from children, brothers from brothers, kin from kin, when – in the *Republic*, once again – he makes the good alone citizens and friends and kin and free (the result is that, on Stoic premisses, parents and children are at enmity: for they are not wise);[3] (3) that he lays down the doctrine, likewise in the *Republic*, that

[1] The Loeb translation of the Diogenes Laertius passages I quote (D.L. VII 32–4, 187–9) is wrong or questionable at various points, especially at D.L. VII 187, where Hicks misinterprets ἀναπλάττει and πινάκων, and 189, where (as I shall argue) his quotation marks are to be dispensed with.

[2] The text seems to require emending here: I follow the Loeb, the OCT, etc. in accepting Reiske's conjecture λέγουσιν for the MSS λέγοντα.

[3] What I present under (2) as a single sentence is treated by the editors (Hicks in the Loeb, Long in the OCT, Gigante in *Diogene Laerzio, Vite dei Filosofi* (Rome–Bari 1987 [2nd edn.])) as two independent clauses, and indeed divided between two distinct paragraphs. On this view 'In the *Republic*, once again...' begins a separate point. But (i) παριστάντα (VII 33) construes more normally as subordinate to λέγειν αὐτόν (VII 32), even if Diogenes Laertius can make a participle the main verb of an independent clause (cf. e.g. κελεύων, λέγων, VII 188, where however we should no doubt understand κατηγορεῖται *vel sim.*). (ii) The clause I bracket ('the result...') is most naturally taken as a consequence primarily of the claim that all who are not good men are at enmity,

> women should be held in common, and (4) (in the 200s) that neither temples nor law-courts nor gymnasia should be built in cities; (5) that on coinage he writes as follows, that 'it must not be thought that coinage should be introduced either for purposes of exchange or for travelling abroad.' And he requires (6) that both men and women should wear the same dress and that no part of the body should be hidden away. That the *Republic* is the work of Zeno Chrysippus also says, in his *On Republic*. And (7) he has discussed erotic topics at the beginning of the work entitled *The Art of Love* but also writes much the same in *Conversations*.[4]
>
> These are the sorts of thing one finds in Cassius, but also in Isidorus the Pergamene rhetorician, who adds that the passages criticized among the Stoics were cut out of the books by Athenodorus the Stoic, who was in charge of the library at Pergamum, and that afterwards they were set in opposition,[5] after Athenodorus had been caught and charged. So much on the passages of Zeno which have been judged spurious.

Although the provisions about coinage and dress are not specifically ascribed to the *Republic*, it seems highly probable that they too belong to that work: Diogenes has simply tired of repeating 'in the *Republic*' again and again. The references to Cassius at the beginning and end of the main part of the report, and the uniform style of the citation of doctrines in the *Republic*, suggest that all the *Republic* material derives ultimately from Cassius.

Later in his Stoic book (at VII 187–9) Diogenes completes his biography of Chrysippus with an account of criticisms made of

even if they are parents and children. There is a syllogism:

> If parents and children are not good/wise, they are at enmity.
> Parents and children are not good/wise.
> Therefore they are at enmity.

The correct punctuation is adopted by H.C. Baldry, 'Zeno's Ideal State', *JHS* 79 (1959) 3–15, at p. 4.

4 On the meanings of διατριβαί see J. Glucker, *Antiochus and the Late Academy* (Göttingen 1978), 162–6.

5 I retain the MSS ἀντιτεθῆναι, as do e.g. Long, Hicks and Gigante. But Hicks ('replaced') and Gigante ('inseriti') translate as though they read ἀνατεθῆναι (Richards). For discussion of the ἀντίθεσις in question see Sections II and IV below.

his book, just as our text completes the biography of Zeno. In a brilliant article of 1879 Wachsmuth made the convincing guess that the critique of Chrysippus derives from the same source as the material on Zeno.[6] I therefore present a translation of this passage also, so that we may have in front of us the whole of the relevant material:

> There are those who run down Chrysippus as having written many things that are disgusting and unspeakable. For (8) in his work *On the ancient natural philosophers* he invents a disgusting story relating to Hera and Zeus, saying in the 600s things nobody who had the misfortune to soil his lips[7] would say. For he makes up this absolutely disgusting story, they say, which is more appropriate to prostitutes than to gods, even if he praises it as a piece of physics – when it is not even recorded by those who have written on pictures. It is not to be found in Polemo or Hypsicrates, and not even in Antigonus. It is invented by him. (9) In *On Republic* he says to have sexual intercourse with mothers and daughters and sons; and he says the same things also in *On things not to be chosen for their own sakes*, right at the beginning. (10) He is also criticized for advising the eating of the dead in the third book of *On Justice* in the 1000s, and (11) for saying in the second book of *On Life and Making a Living* that we should consider how the wise man is to make his living.[8] Yet for what purpose should he make a living? If for the sake of life, life is an indifferent; if for pleasure, that too is indifferent; if for virtue, that is suffi-

[6] C. Wachsmuth, 'Stichometrisches und Bibliothekarisches', *Rh. Mus.* 34 (1879) 38–51, at pp. 39–42. The point has recently been freshly argued, without reference to Wachsmuth's paper, by J. Mansfeld, 'Diogenes Laertius on Stoic Philosophy', *Elenchos* 7 (1986) 297–382, at pp. 344–6. I have learned an enormous amount about doxography from Mansfeld's article, as indeed from other publications of his.

[7] This is presumably an allusion to the act of fellatio which was the subject of the picture Chrysippus claimed to be interpreting (*SVF* II 1072–4: Clement, Theophilus, Origen).

[8] Von Arnim (*SVF* III 685, app. crit.) says that the otherwise unattested title περὶ βίου καὶ πορισμοῦ is a scholarly fiction. It is in fact what the MSS give us, and von Arnim therefore has to emend to achieve a different title (περὶ βίων). The received text (followed here) is supported by Hesychius *Vir. Illust.* 78: Χρύσιππον τὸν φιλόσοφον αἰτιῶνταί τινες προνοεῖν λέγοντα, ὅπως ποριστέον τῷ σοφῷ.

> cient by itself for happiness. The methods of making a living he recommends are also ludicrous: e.g. being maintained by a king, since he will have to defer to him; or by friends, since friendship will then be bought for gain; or living by his wisdom, for wisdom will then become mercenary. These are the objections that are made.

The reason for thinking that these two passages really constitute a single body of material divided into separate bits by Diogenes Laertius is not just that (a) they occur at similar places in his lives of Zeno and Chrysippus, as critical appendixes to the main accounts. More telling is (b) the citing of doctrines in specific treatises (*laudationes*) not merely by title or book and title, but by position within a book, indicated either by 'at the beginning' or by a rough line reference: the 200s, the 600s, the 1000s,[9] or (in (2) above) by reference to a major point in the work in question: 'when he makes the good alone citizens, etc.'[10] The specification of line references with respect to works of prose appears to be almost unique in classical literature.[11] (c) Both passages display arcane

[9] Mansfeld (*Elenchos* 7 (1986) 297–382, at pp. 345–6) and Gigante (*Diogene Laerzio*, pp. 255, 311) take the expressions κατὰ τοὺς χιλίους στίχους etc. as meaning 'at *a length of* 1000 lines' etc. rather than 'somewhere between line 1000 and line 1100' etc. It is true that this translation gives a good point: Zeno and Chrysippus developed these themes at considerable length, so criticism of their views is fully justified. But it appears to neglect the definite article τούς; and the mention of στίχοι (lines) takes us into a vocabulary elsewhere employed to make relatively precise *references* to particular passages within the book in which they occur (see further n. 11 below). The point of such references in our texts would presumably be mostly to try to enhance the scholarly authority of the critique of Stoicism they contain. Wachsmuth (42–3) makes an unconvincing attempt to connect them with Athenodorus' bowdlerizing activities.

[10] It is not so clear that in (2) (D.L. VII 33) we have a passage identified by position in the book as it is in all the other cases (i.e. (1), (4), (8), (9), (10)); but comparison with the wording employed in them indicates that this is certainly a possibility – and gives the reference to Zeno's thesis about the good a definite point it would otherwise lack. A translation which would bring the point out more sharply would be: 'once again in the *Republic*, in the passage where he makes the good alone citizens ...'

[11] It is one of only five such texts to make such references, according to K. Ohly, *Stichometrische Untersuchungen* (Leipzig 1928), 109–17; the others being Asconius' commentaries on Cicero, a scholiast on Oribasius (referring to various works of Galen), Eustathius on Origen (referring to St John's Gospel), and Hegemonius against the Manichees. It emerges that the word στίχος in such contexts serves as a term of art, applied to prose works on the analogy of the verse line in poetry. Because scribes writing out prose texts observed no standard length of line, there developed a convention whereby references to prose

bibliographical learning. At VII 187 this takes the form of a little disquisition on paintings or mythological subjects for paintings; at VII 34 information about the activities of Athenodorus at Pergamum. (d) In both cases mentioned under (c), there in fact appears to be a strong Pergamene connection. For as Wilamowitz showed, the Antigonus mentioned in VII 187, who is probably to be identified with the third century B.C. biographer Antigonus of Carystus, seems likely to have been active in Pergamum as a sculptor in the service of Attalus I.[12] The work of his to which VII 187 refers may well have been composed in Pergamum also: where better could one put together a book about paintings than in a good library?

D.L. VII 32–4 and 187–9 therefore originally formed a single critique of Zeno and Chrysippus. Isidorus (or someone who excerpts Isidorus) is presumably Diogenes' source. But behind Isidorus lies Cassius, not just at VII 32–4, but also at VII 187–9. For if Cassius is responsible for the line reference to Zeno's *Republic*, he is likely to have been responsible for the line references to Chrysippus, too, and with them for the Chrysippus material in general. The only thing that Isidorus may have contributed in the Chrysippus section, matching his bibliographical information about Athenodorus, is the allegation that writers on painting

authors *assumed* a standard length, generally reckoned (on the model of the hexameter) as 15 or 16 syllables (cf. H. Diels, 'Stichometrisches', *Hermes* 17 (1882) 377–84). For a recent summary see G. Cavallo, *Libri scritture scribi a Ercolano*, suppl. I *Cronache Ercolanesi* 13 (1983) 20–2. There is a logical papyrus (P Pariginus 2 = *SVF* II 180 = 1080 Hülser) which has in its margins what are apparently numerals (M, N), to be interpreted as marking 100 line intervals (i.e. conventional standard lines) – presumably 1200 and 1300. For discussion see Ohly, p. 57; photograph in W. Cavini *et al.*, *Studi su papiri greci di logica e medicina* (Florence 1985), 112, with transcripts at pp. 144, 156, and brief discussion (after Ohly) p. 130. I am indebted to Peter Parsons for generous help with the subject of this note.

[12] U. von Wilamowitz-Moellendorff, *Antigonos von Karystos* (Berlin 1881), ch. I. Polemon is likewise a well-known author on painting (among other subjects), who flourished in the first quarter of the 2nd century B.C., and wrote a book *Against Adaeus and Antigonus* often referred to by Athenaeus: see frr. 56–69 of the Polemo section in *FHG* III, and the *RE* article by K. Deichgräber, XXI. 2 1288–1320. On the other hand, no Hypsicrates is otherwise known as an authority on the subject. So on the strength of a reference in Pliny the Elder (*NH* XXXV 68) to 'Antigonus et Xenocrates qui de pictura scripsere', Wilamowitz emended 'Hypsicrates' to 'Xenocrates' (*Antigonos*, p. 8 with n. 3). Gigante (*Diogene Laerzio*, p. 311) follows suit, but the idea has all the weaknesses familiar in arguments from silence (or in this case near-silence).

know nothing about the painting of Zeus and Hera which Chrysippus claimed to be expounding.

II

At first glance one might have been inclined to dismiss the anecdote about Athenodorus recorded at D.L. VII 34 as merely *ben trovato*, or at any rate to suspend belief. In fact the story enables us to make such excellent sense of the philosophical material in D.L. VII 32–3, and coheres so well with other evidence, that we should accept the gist of it as true.

The first thing to notice is that there are two stages in the history told by Isodorus. First, there were various passages in Zeno's works which were criticized by the Stoics themselves. Athenodorus went one step further, and actually excised them from the text. Second, after Athenodorus was found out the passages in question were 'set in opposition' (ἀντιτεθῆναι).

(i) *Who* set them in opposition? (ii) What sort of opposition? (iii) And against what? (i) Cassius has not yet entered Isidorus' account. He is therefore the obvious candidate, as is confirmed by the information that he was a Sceptic. For the method a Pyrrhonian Sceptic employed to arrive at suspension of belief was 'by the setting of things in opposition' (διὰ τῆς ἀντιθέσεως τῶν πραγμάτων, *PH* I 31 *et passim*; cf. D.L. IX 74–6, 78). (ii) If (i) is on the right lines, 'set in opposition' is a reference to standard Pyrrhonist technique. Indeed the laconic use of the expression ἀντιτεθῆναι here is the more intelligible if we assume that Diogenes Laertius expects the reader to appreciate a technical term. (iii) Given (i) and (ii) it is natural to assume that Cassius set passages of Zeno in opposition to *other* Stoic texts, thus establishing a Stoic self-contradiction, and showing that a Stoic in particular will inevitably find himself suspending belief on the topics of the passages in question. It is not explicitly stated what the Zeno passages Athenodorus objected to were or that he included those listed in §§32–3, but this is a natural way to read §34, and required of us if (i) is accepted.

So Isidorus implies that two quite different sorts of criticism were levelled at Zeno. The Stoics themselves found certain parts of the *Republic* objectionable. Cassius the Sceptic then used the same passages to create one side of an anti-Stoic antinomy.

Other evidence tends to confirm both elements in this account.

III

There happens to be some evidence of Athenodorus' date. Plutarch (*Cato minor* 10; cf. *de princ. philos.* 777 A, Strabo XIV 5.14) has a story of how Cato the younger, while on service as military tribune in Macedonia (67-6 B.C.), took the opportunity of a vacation to visit Athenodorus Cordylion the Stoic, already an old man, in Pergamum. Although Athenodorus had the reputation of being uncommunicative, the two are reported to have got on famously. This is presumably our Athenodorus.[13] His attempts to clean up Zeno would then probably belong to the early years of the first century B.C.

Such a date coheres satisfyingly with our other main piece of evidence about later Stoic embarrassment over earlier Stoic writings, above all Zeno's *Republic*. This is supplied by a work partially preserved in the Herculaneum papyri: Philodemus' *On the Stoics*.[14] Philodemus seems to have been a fairly exact contemporary of Cicero, and his literary production, like Cicero's, probably spans at least the second quarter of the first century B.C. *On the Stoics* takes as its focus Stoic attempts to explain away the indecencies or apparent indecencies of Zeno's *Republic*: e.g. that it was a flawed juvenile work, not the real Zeno; that it was real Zeno all right, but Stoics want to be thought of as essentially Socratics – they acknowledge Zeno's authority only on account of his doctrine about the τέλος or goal of life, not because of anything in *Republic*; that the teaching of the *Republic* is impeccable – although its line on sexual intercourse needs explanation. At one

[13] So *RE* II 2045 s.v. Athenodoros (18). Cf. the list of Stoics contained in some MSS of Diogenes Laertius, who were presumably dealt with in the lost part of D.L. VII: reproduced e.g. in Gigante, *Diogene Laerzio*, p. CXVI; L. Edelstein and I.G. Kidd, *Posidonius* vol. I (Cambridge 1972), T 66.

[14] See the editions of W. Crönert, *Kolotes und Menedemos* (Munich 1906), 53–67, still indispensable for its separate presentation of the information in the two papyri in question (P. Herc. 155 and 339); and T. Dorandi, 'Filodemo, Gli Stoici (P. Herc. 155 e 339)', *Cron. Erc.* 12 (1982) 91–133.

point Philodemus refers to 'some of our contemporaries' (τινες τῶν καθ' ἡμᾶς, col. XV 13), so at any rate some of the Stoic arguments he attacks originate in his own time. What these 'contemporaries' are apparently attempting to rebut is the charge that Zeno is a Cynic in his teaching. Their tactic is to deny that Diogenes ever wrote a *Republic* – and hence (presumably) that he held any doctrines for Zeno to borrow (col. XV 14ff.; cf. D.L. VI 80, 103).[15] Whether the other Stoic defences of Zeno Philodemus considers are also contemporary is not clear.[16]

What did Athenodorus find embarrassing in the parts of the *Republic* he excised? The list of doctrines set down in D.L. VII 32–3 is of course in the first instance geared to *Cassius*' line of attack, not Athenodorus'; or so for the moment it is prudent to assume. In any event the text is notably unforthcoming on *what* was considered problematic about them. Nonetheless there is a strong case for seeing their similarity to Cynic teaching as the common strand. This makes it tempting to guess[17] that what Athenodorus was trying to eradicate from Zeno's book was any trace of Cynicism, presumably because he regarded it as antinomian. In that case it may have been, in part at least, Athenodorus' activities which called forth the response Philodemus attributes to 'some of our contemporaries'.

Here is the argument for a Cynic focus in D.L. VII 32–3:

(1) *General education.* In declaring general education useless, Zeno put himself in the same camp as the Cynics as they are represented in the doxography in Diogenes Laertius (VI 103–4).[18] This is one of the rare questions on which (according to our

[15] Philodemus' refutation of this line of argument (col. XV 16-XVII fin.), depending mostly on references to Diogenes' *Republic* in Cleanthes and Chrysippus, is to my mind entirely convincing. Most modern scholars agree. For recent surveys of the issue see G. Giannantoni, *Socraticorum Reliquiae* (Rome 1985), vol. III, pp. 416–17; M.-O. Goulet-Cazé, *L'Ascèse Cynique* (Paris 1986), pp. 85–90.

[16] The names of Panaetius or of Stoics who may belong to the generation succeeding him such as Stratocles of Rhodes and Apollonius of Tyre have been suggested as Philodemus' targets: see Goulet-Cazé, *L'Ascèse Cynique*, p. 89.

[17] So Mansfeld, 'Diogenes Laertius on Stoic Philosophy', *Elenchos* 7 (1986) 297–382, at pp. 344, 346.

[18] On which see Mansfeld, *Elenchos* 7 (1986) 297–382, at pp. 328–351; M.-O. Goulet-Cazé, 'Un syllogisme Stoicien sur la loi dans la doxographie de Diogène le Cynique', *Rh. Mus.* 125 (1982) 214–40, at pp. 233–5.

evidence) Chrysippus contradicted Zeno (VII 129). A later Stoic would accordingly have reason to want to delete the passage where Zeno took the Cynicizing line he did, given that Chrysippus' view was presumably the one that prevailed in the school.

(2) *Friendship and enmity.* Let us suppose that friendship and enmity was the theme in Zeno's account of the sage on which Athenodorus, as well as Cassius, fastened. Then there are sufficient Cynic antecedents for Zeno's position, at any rate as Diogenes Laertius presents Cynicism.[19] Several of the aphorisms ascribed by Diocles[20] to Antisthenes (who of course figures as the

[19] Mansfeld has established that in the Hellenistic period there developed 'two different views concerned with the continuity between Cynics and Stoics, viz. one (the tradition preferred by Diog. Laert.) emphasizing dignified ethics, the other (sort of tucked away by him [i.e. mainly in VII 32–4, 187–9]) immoral and obscene ideas' (*Elenchos* 7 [1986] 346). It might therefore be thought unlikely that Athenodorus should associate Zeno's views on friends and enemies with the dignified version of Cynicism: was the dignified version not constructed precisely in order to make the antecedents of Stoicism respectable, not something requiring the censoring of the relevant elements of Stoic doctrine? But Athenodorus would not necessarily have supposed that e.g. Diocles' Antisthenes was safely sanitized from a Stoic point of view. He might rather have found his views on friendship and kinsmen as threateningly antinomian as Diogenes' on relations between the sexes – even though the one position might be thought to err in being too stringent, the other in being too lax in its demands. It is important to remember the huge importance of the king's friends in the Hellenistic monarchies: see e.g. F.W. Walbank, 'Monarchies and monarchic ideas', in *The Cambridge Ancient History*, 2nd edition, vol. VII.1, ed. Walbank *et al.* (Cambridge 1984), 68–71. No court could have survived application of Antisthenes' principles. Nor indeed could Hellenistic diplomacy, in which the forming of 'friendships' played an equally large role: E. Gruen, *The Hellenistic World and the Coming of Rome* I (Berkeley and Los Angeles, 1984), ch. 2. To conclude, antinomian moralities are generally ambiguous: 'Love God and do what you like' is both an uncommonly rigorous and an uncommonly permissive injunction; Mansfeld's opposition of 'dignified' and 'immoral' cannot in the end be pressed too hard.

[20] On Diocles of Magnesia see further e.g. J. Meyer, *Diogenes Laertius and his Hellenistic Background* (Wiesbaden 1978), 42–5. He is usually given a date early in the first century B.C. on the strength of a highly speculative and indeed flimsy argument by E. Maass, *De Biographis Graecis Quaestiones Selectae* (Berlin 1880) 8–23, at pp. 16–19. The question is further complicated by disagreement among scholars over the extent of the quotation from Diocles made by Diogenes Laertius in his account of Stoic logic (VII 49 ff.): see e.g. Mansfeld, *Elenchos* 7 (1986) 351–73. I myself incline to the view that only VII 49–53 come from Diocles. In which case no philosopher later than Chrysippus is mentioned by Diocles as reported by Diogenes Laertius, and nothing stands in the way of a date around 200 B.C. for his literary activity. There would then be no particular difficulty in supposing that Athenodorus Cordylion knew his collection of Antisthenean sayings (probably in Diocles' *Lives of the Philosophers*: so

proto-Cynic in D.L. VI) read like pre-echoes of Zeno (D.L. VI 12): 'The morally good are friends. Make allies of those who are at once courageous and just ... It is better to fight with a few good men against all the bad than with many bad men against a few good ... Rate the just man higher than a kinsman ... Consider all that is morally bad to be foreign.' Athenodorus, like Plutarch subsequently, might well have found it hard to reconcile this rigorous doctrine with the theory of οἰκείωσις, particularly where each has implications for the relations of parents with their children. For the theory claims that nature drives parents to love their offspring – good or bad, presumably (e.g. Cic. *Fin.* III 62; cf. Plu. *Stoic. rep.* 1038 A–B).

(3) *Women in common.* In some sense or other Diogenes the Cynic had advocated that 'women be held in common, recognizing no convention of marriage, but taking the view that a man and a woman should live with each other provided only that they persuade each other[21] (and for this reason he thought that sons too should be held in common)' (D.L. VI 72). Zeno's endorsement of the idea was itself endorsed by Chrysippus, in his own *On Republic* (D.L. VII 131). Athenodorus would no doubt have wished to pay more attention to the Stoic doctrine that in most circumstances the sage will participate in political and social life in general and in particular take a wife and have children (D.L. VII 121, Stob. II 109. 10–20, Cic. *Fin.* III 68): it is appropriate (οἰκεῖον) for the good man "to (con)descend (συγκαταβαίνειν) both to marriage and to having children, both for himself and for his country" (Stob. II 94. 13–15).

(4) *Prohibition on public buildings.* I postpone discussion of this item to (6) below.

(5) *Abolition of coinage.* The slogan: 'Deface the coinage' is presented as a key element in the teaching of Diogenes of Sinope in both the biographical and the doxographical sections of the

Mansfeld, *Elenchos* 7 (1986) 305 nn. 13 and 14). But as librarian in Pergamum he may of course have read the original Cynic sources, including Antisthenes, for himself.

21 I read πεισάσῃ with the MSS, emended in line with conventional sexist ideology rejected by Diogenes to πεισθείσῃ by Stephanus, who is generally followed by modern editors. I cannot pretend to have thought of abandoning the emendation myself: see G.B. Donzelli, 'Un' ideologia "contestataria" del secolo IV A.C.', *SIFC* 42 (1970) 225–51, at p. 227 n. 2.

life in D.L. VI (20–1, 71). And we have independent evidence that *his Republic* advocated the use of knucklebones as coins (Athen. IV 159 C, Phld. *On the Stoics*, col. XVI 6–9 D). Coinage was a metaphor for all conventions: all were to be disregarded or flouted, since they stand in the way of the life according to nature and shackle our freedom (D.L. VI 71).[22] If Athenodorus was determined to remove Cynic elements from Zeno's *Republic* as antinomian, his doctrine on coinage was a prime candidate for excision.

(6) *Rules on dress.* What immediately marked out a Cynic was his dress: he doubled his cloak, which was his one garment, and added only a staff and a wallet (e.g. D.L. VI 13). Zeno's unisex instruction (cf. Phld. *On the Stoics* col. XIX 12–14) recalls Hipparchia's notorious habit of wearing the cloak (τρίβων) like her husband Crates (D.L. VI 93, 97). The injunction that no part of the body should be hidden away (i.e. when doing athletics, Phld. *On the Stoics* col. XIX 17–22) reminds us that Diogenes is alleged to 'have done everything in public' (D.L. VI 69), even if the echoes of Plato's *Republic* are stronger (452 A–B, 457 A–B). In the case of item (6), then, as of (1) to (3) and (5), it seems probable that Athenodorus' excision was motivated by the desire to get rid of anything that could be construed as Cynic. This conclusion prompts the guess that item (4) requires the same sort of explanation, even though we have no specific evidence of Cynic opinion on its subject.[23] The abolition of temples, lawcourts and gymnasia constitutes an assault on the central institutions of political life as ordinarily understood. So the sort of nervousness Athenodorus will have felt about this antinomian proposal of Zeno's is surely a close cousin of the abhorrence of Cynic ideas and practices which, as I have argued, must have inspired his attitude to all the other items on the list.

[22] I follow what I take to be the prevailing modern reading of Diogenes' slogan: see e.g. H. Diels, 'Aus dem Leben des Cynikers Diogenes', *AGP* 7 (1894) 313–16; K. von Fritz, *Quellenuntersuchungen zu Leben und Philosophie des Diogenes von Sinope* (Leipzig 1926), pp. 19–20. There is now a comprehensive study of the whole topic in G. Giannantoni, *Socraticorum Reliquiae*, vol. III (Rome 1985), pp. 379–88.

[23] The doxography at D.L. VI 73 says that according to Diogenes there was nothing out of place in taking something from a temple. But that falls some way short of Zeno's comprehensive radicalism.

IV

In order to get to grips with Cassius' use of Athenodorus' passages from Zeno, we need first to move away from the summary at D.L. VII 32–3. Elsewhere we find something which looks much closer to being an actual extract from Cassius. There is in *PH* III 245–8 and *M* XI 189–94 a virtually identical sequence of verbatim snippets from Zeno and Chrysippus, introduced by Sextus in connection with the topic: 'Is there an art of living?' (εἰ ἔστι τέχνη περὶ τὸν βίον, to quote the formulation in *PH*). The passages are not typical Sextus. He makes great play here of the fact that these are verbatim quotations from specified works of Zeno and Chrysippus, when *PH* as a whole contains very little explicitly advertised quotation, and *M* does not elsewhere quote from the Stoics or Epicureans in such fashion (although for example the famous section in *M* VII on Democritus and the criterion of truth is in this style). The natural inference is that Sextus is just reproducing material from a source written not in his own usual manner.

The items Sextus cites are as follows:

(a) An excerpt from Zeno's *Conversations* on sexual intercourse with one's boy-friend. In *M* XI, but not in *PH* III, this is followed by a further excerpt on the same topic, presumably also from *Conversations*.[24]

(b) An extract from an unnamed work of Zeno to the effect that (as Sextus puts it) there was nothing terrible in Oedipus' having sex with his mother Jocasta.

(c) An extract from Chrysippus' *Republic* on incest.

(d) A quotation from Chrysippus' *On Justice* introduced to prove that the Stoics approved of eating people – 'not only the dead [as *M* XI puts it], but our own flesh, if ever a part of the body should happen to be cut off'.

(e) The longest quotation in the set, from a discussion in Chrysippus' *On Appropriate Action* on the burial of parents, which also suggests using their flesh – and our own limbs if amputated – as food, provided it is edible.

[24] The Loeb translator fails to recognize a book title here (*PH* III 245, *M* XI 190): Διατριβαί, *Conversations*, i.e. the same work as is mentioned at D.L. VII 34.

There is an impressive degree of correlation with the list of Stoic doctrines which according to Diogenes Laertius came under fire from critics. (a) here corresponds with (7) in the list in D.L. VII, (c) with (9), and (d) with (10). Since (e) simply covers the same ground as (d) its non-appearance in Diogenes Laertius hardly constitutes a very substantial omission. Notice that the two lists present their material in the same order, disturbed only by the inclusion in Diogenes Laertius of (8) between (7) and (9) and the omission of (b). Notice also that Sextus' list straddles what, according to our argument, are the two parts of Cassius' list, thus confirming that it was originally a single list.[25]

There is a principle of organization governing Sextus' list, which he spells out explicitly in the introduction at *M* XI 189:

> For example, since many things are said by the Stoics about the education of children, and about the honour due to parents, and again about piety towards the departed, we shall select a few of them under each head and produce them by way of example in order to develop our argument.

(a), which concerns conduct towards one's παιδικά, i.e. the boy one is 'in love with', supplies examples of the Stoic view of education; (b) and (c) of respect to parents; (d) and (e) of piety to the departed. Both the *PH* and the *M* accounts indicate that this is what the examples are examples of, as they present them.

If now we return to D.L. VII 32–3 a striking fact is immediately apparent. Point (1) on its list of Zenonian doctrines has to do with education, point (2) with parents and children. Thus on the composite list constructed from the two Diogenes Laertius passages, at least *two* items, viz. (1) and (7) [=(a)], dealt or were construed as dealing with education, and *two* also with parents and children, viz. (2) and (9) [=(c)] (plus, of course, (b) on Sextus' list).

Recall next that in Section II we concluded that what Cassius did with the extracts from Zeno's *Republic* which embarrassed the Stoics was set them in opposition to *other* Stoic texts. Are (7) [=(a)] and (9) [=(c)] plus (b) plausibly interpreted as *opposed* to (1) and (2)? Certainly in the case of the parent–child relation there

[25] So Mansfeld, *Elenchos* 7 (1986) 346 n. 105.

are grounds for an affirmative answer.[26] For if the *Republic* implies that parents and children are bound to be at enmity with each other (unless all involved are sages), Zeno's acceptance of the incest of Oedipus and Jocasta and Chrysippus' endorsement of sex between parents and children in *On Republic* seem to go to the opposite extreme.

The possibility of an opposition between (2) and (9) prompts a more systematic consideration of the relationship between the *Republic* doctrines mentioned in D.L. VII 32–3 and the other Zenonian and Chrysippean material in the Diogenes Laertius passages and in Sextus. The table of correspondences is easily constructed:

	Republic	Other Stoic texts
Education	(1)	(7) [= (a)], (8)
Parent/child	(2)	(9) [= (c)], (b)
Women in common	(3)	—
Piety	(4)	(10) [= (d)], (e)
Money	(5)	(11)
Dress	(6)	—

In the case of (5) and (11) there is an obvious possibility of opposition: whereas Zeno is so antipathetic to private possessions that he abolishes money altogether, Chrysippus devotes energy to the question of how the sage should acquire money and possessions. With (4) and (10) it is probably fair to say that the sense of a contradiction between them is scarcely ineluctable, but is nonetheless not hard to contrive. (4), as it stands, of course, does not look as though it is specially oriented towards religion. But it seems not unlikely that the extract from Zeno which was used to illustrate the point is one preserved in a number of Christian authors (cf. *SVF* I 264 and 265) as well as in Plutarch. For texts

[26] It is no objection that a Stoic could easily show that on his principles this is no contradiction, e.g. because talk about indifferents must be distinguished from talk about good and bad. For he could as easily dispose of many of the contradictions and like difficulties alleged by Plutarch in *Stoic. rep.* and *Comm. not.*, e.g. in *Stoic. rep.* 18. 1042 A ff. and 30. 1047 E ff.

giving Zeno's *ipsissima verba* are rarely to be found, yet in the case of his views on temples Clement gives a verbatim quotation specifically attributed to the *Republic* (*Strom.* v 12, 76). It seems economical to suppose that his source is Cassius (directly or indirectly). Clement's quotation is unfortunately garbled, as Cherniss points out in his translation of Plutarch's version (ad loc.), which gets the sense right if not the exact wording (*Stoic. rep.* 1034 B):

> Moreover, it is a doctrine of Zeno's not to build temples of the gods, because a temple not worth much is also not sacred, and no work of builders or manual workers is worth much.

Armed with the Zenonian original of this report, Cassius might well have argued that, whereas Zeno in the *Republic* shows himself extraordinarily purist in matters of piety, Chrysippus in *On Justice* and *On Appropriate Action* reveals no scruples whatever. Finally, it would at any rate be consistent with the account of the other correspondences we have given to postulate a similar opposition between (1) and (7) and (8). Cassius might have said: Zeno in the *Republic* high-mindedly rejects traditional education as unprofitable; but in *Conversations* he has so little concern for education that he recommends debauching one's pupils, and Chrysippus not only rehabilitates Homer and Hesiod (staples of the ordinary curriculum) but engages in some obscene mythopoeic invention on his own account. (Since Sextus does not refer to (8) we can only guess that Cassius included it in his education section. Its place between (7) and (9) suggests this hypothesis; and its relevance to education seems no weaker than (7)'s.) Why no correspondences for (3) and (6)? Various possible explanations come to mind. But Cassius' strategy as we have reconstructed it consists in portraying the *Republic* as morally elevated in comparison with the unrestrained self-indulgence and moral banality exemplified in other Stoic texts. The provisions of the *Republic* on women and dress would not have fitted very smoothly into such a system of contrasts. So, I conjecture, Cassius did not try to find correspondences with them.

The hypothesis that the Stoic material in D.L. vii 32–3 and 187–8 was originally presented by Cassius in the form of an antithesis designed to exhibit a sequence of self-contradictions might on first hearing seem unduly speculative. Yet we have done little more than use the text and related matter in Sextus to work out in detail the interpretation of Cassius' strategy already argued in Section II. In particular, we have seen how the hypothesis enunciates a formal structure which comfortably accommodates both the items of Stoic doctrine discussed in Diogenes Laertius and Sextus and the order in which they are presented. We can add that it enables us to account for features of both texts which would otherwise remain mysterious. Thus in Sextus one would be hard pressed to offer a reason why the material from Zeno's *Conversations* on having sex with boy-friends should be put forward as an illustration of Stoic views on *education*. The hypothesis can explain that Cassius needed Stoic passages which could more or less plausibly be opposed to the explicit doctrine about education proposed in the *Republic*. Again, in D.L. VII 187–8 it would be difficult otherwise to understand why, after a catalogue of Chrysippean passages obviously open to criticism as morally disgusting, the text concludes with passage (11) on making a living: a topic apparently quite disconnected. The hypothesis can once again appeal to Cassius' need for Stoic material to oppose to the view of money taken in the *Republic*.

It is worth dwelling on the discussion of (11) in D.L. VII 189, for it is almost the only section of text in either Diogenes Laertius or Sextus where Cassius' lines of argument are preserved. Editors have curiously supposed that VII 189 is a quotation from Chrysippus rather than an objection to him, although it is not Diogenes' habit to introduce long verbatim prose quotations from original Stoic authors in Book VII, nor is there clear or indeed any indication here that he is breaking his habit, and although Hesychius, when copying the passage out for the final chapter of *de viris illustribus*, takes it as an objection to Chrysippus.[27] I take it to be

[27] The passage is presented as a quotation in the Loeb and in the OCT. Von Arnim (*SVF* III 685) and Gigante are more cautious, but both take it as at least a summary of a pair of Chrysippean arguments. Hesychius, on the other hand, having said that some people criticize Chrysippus for saying that we should consider how the sage is to make a living, continues: φασὶ γάρ· τίνος χάριν ποριστέον αὐτῷ; ('For *they say*: for what purpose should he make a living?' *Vir. Illust.* 78).

obvious that it is a critique of his well-attested doctrine that for the wise man there are three preferred ways of acquiring property: from kingship, from political society and particularly his friends in politics, and from philosophy.[28] There are two objections. First, on the Stoics' own premisses there can be no point in making a living if one is a sage: to be alive, or again pleasure – things that ordinary people aim for – are indifferent in his eyes; virtue, which he *does* count good, is sufficient itself for happiness (money or a full stomach does not enter into his calculations). Second, all the ways of making a living Chrysippus holds to be preferred are ludicrous: ludicrous, presumably, if one holds elevated moral views as the Stoics do, since in each case the sage is required to act as though he held much more mercenary or slavish views. As soon as this second line of argument is concluded, we are told: 'These are the objections that are made.' This statement is not restricted to the objections to Chrysippus' doctrine on making a living which have just been raised, but must surely include them within its scope. Moreover, there was a special reason why in the case of this doctrine Diogenes Laertius should spell out the argument against Chrysippus in detail: anybody can see that there is something objectionable in his doctrines about incest and eating the dead, whereas the impropriety of the

[28] Cf. Stob. II 109.10 ff. = *SVF* III 686; Plu. *Stoic. rep.* 1043 E = *SVF* III 693. W.W. Tarn ('Alexander, Cynics and Stoics', *AJP* 60 (1939) 41–70, at pp. 60–1) thought Chrysippus' espousal of this doctrine 'savagely sarcastic', because 'the Stoic σοφός in Stoic eyes has no business to want' to make money. But wealth and being alive are things 'preferred' according to a Stoic doctrine (D.L. VII 106) which in its fundamental points goes back to Zeno (Stob. II 84.18 ff.). That is no doubt why among all his other attributes the sage is to be a χρηματιστικός or expert in acquiring possessions: the only true χρηματιστικός (Stob. II 95.10, 14–23). Tarn takes Stob. II 109.10 ff. (and would no doubt have taken II 95.14–23 similarly) as a late Stoic attempt to mitigate the unworldliness of the early Stoa, and Plutarch as missing the sarcasm in what Chrysippus said. Insofar as this interpretation does not simply fail to reckon with the doctrine of what is preferred, it rests on the claim that Chrysippus' description of making a living from philosophy as σοφιστεύειν (e.g. Stob. II 109.20 ff., Plu. *Stoic. rep.* 1047 F) decisively reveals his contempt for the whole business of money-making: which is false, since Stobaeus' text shows that the Stoics argued precisely over whether σοφιστεύειν had this implication or not. And his final support is our text, D.L. VII 189, which he naturally construes as Chrysippus, not an objection to Chrysippus. Tarn's discussion is well worth consulting just because it expresses clearly and trenchantly the philosophical motivation for construing the text as the editors do.

sage's making a living needs explanation – an explanation which turns out to involve a charge of Stoic self-contradiction.

V

Section II observed that Isidorus' story implies first Stoic criticism of passages in Zeno's *Republic* followed by Sceptic use of those same passages to demonstrate that the Stoics contradict themselves. Examination of the relevant texts in Diogenes Laertius and Sextus in Sections III and IV has confirmed this part of the story. Isidorus further claimed that the *Republic* passages 'were set in opposition after Athenodorus had been caught and charged'. This suggests that Cassius' critique was a contemporaneous response to the embarrassment of the Stoics with regard to the *Republic*. Should we accept the suggestion?

It would certainly be compatible with what we have seen of Cassius' technique in Section IV to suppose that he was arguing: (1) The Stoics cannot disclaim Zeno's *Republic*, for it is attested as Zeno's by Chrysippus himself. (2) The doctrines in the *Republic* they are embarrassed by may indeed be objectionable. (3) But elsewhere in Stoicism we can find contradictory doctrines which are no less objectionable. (4) So why bowdlerize the *Republic* as Athenodorus attempted to do? The natural outcome from consideration of (2) and (3) together is suspension of belief. We cannot assume that Cassius' argument *did* go just like that. But the sting in his critique will have been much sharper if it exploited the fact that the passages of the *Republic* he fastened on disconcerted contemporary Stoics themselves.

So it is tempting to make Cassius Athenodorus' contemporary.[29] The first half of the first century B.C. is clearly the time when controversy about Zeno's *Republic* was at its height. Salvos were fired from places as far apart as Pergamum and Herculaneum. If any moment was ripe to make capital out of the detection

[29] M. Dal Pra, *Lo Scetticismo Greco* (Rome-Bari 1975 [2nd edn.]), pp. 456–7, guesses that Cassius is a contemporary of Menodotus of Nicomedia (whom he dates to the first half of the second century A.D.), presumably because Galen mentions him in the same context as Menodotus, in a way which could but does not necessarily suggest that he was disagreeing with ideas already put forward by him (*Subfig. emp.*, pp. 49.26–50.1 D).

of Athenodorus' bibliographical crime, it was soon after the event – before the whole business of the excisions had turned into a mere anecdote, and the arguments and anxieties gone cold, which prompted him to act and Philodemus and his Stoic adversaries to write.[30]

Cassius was a Pyrrhonist: that is the only thing that could be meant by the designation 'sceptic' at D.L. VII 32. It is in all probability confirmed by Galen *Subfig. emp.* 4, pp. 49. 29 ff. D, where we are told that Cassius the Pyrrhonian held that the empiricist doctor does not use even transition from like to like in his diagnosis. Does Cassius' Pyrrhonist allegiance rule out so early a date? Surely not. Aenesidemus broke with the new Academy to become the reviver of Pyrrhonism at just this time.[31] It would be pleasant to think that in Cassius we had found an early follower of his and indeed perhaps a companion-in-arms.

[30] I refrain from speculation on the date of Isidorus, who is placed in the time of Cicero at *RE* IX 2064 (presumably following Wilamowitz in his *Epistula ad Maass* (Berlin 1880), p. 161), on the flimsy basis of a reference to an Isidorus in Rutilius Lupus II 16, an epitome of a rhetorical treatise by Cicero's contemporary, Gorgias of Athens.

[31] See e.g. M. Dal Pra, *Lo Scetticismo Greco*, pp. 351–4; J. Glucker, *Antiochus and the Late Academy*, pp. 116–18.

2

City of love

I

What was Zeno's principal political proposal in the *Republic*? Three possibilities may occur to the reader of Diogenes Laertius' report at VII 32–3:

(a) *Antinomianism.* No positive political ideal emerges or is intended to emerge. The spirit of Zeno's recommendations is altogether critical and antinomian.[1]

(b) *Revisionism.* Zeno does indicate a positive ideal: a community of sages. But it represents a radically revised conception of community, for what is envisaged is a society made up of the wise and good alone, wherever they are on the face of the earth. They belong to it and indeed make it a society simply because they are a plurality of persons characterized by wisdom and goodness.[2]

(c) *Communism.* The ideal is a community as ordinarily conceived, i.e. a body of people constituted as such by contingent circumstances like physical proximity and mutual acquaintance (among other things). In some sense it embraces children and adolescents as well as mature adults. What makes Zeno's community ideal is the degree of concord achieved in it through the political virtue of its citizens, which is in turn fostered by communist political institutions.[3]

[1] This is the view of e.g. M.I. Finley, 'Utopianism Ancient and Modern', in *The Use and Abuse of History* (London 1975), at p. 188.

[2] See A. Erskine, *The Hellenistic Stoa* (London 1990), pp. 18–27; cf. A.-J. Voelke, *Les Rapports avec autrui dans la philosophie grecque* (Paris 1961), pp. 123ff.

[3] The best statement of this interpretation is by H.C. Baldry, 'Zeno's ideal state', *JHS* 79 (1959) 3–15: an excellent article to which I am much indebted.

I shall comment briefly on these alternatives and their philosophical affiliations.

Reading (a) will appeal to those struck by the affinities between the ideas ascribed to Zeno at D.L. VII 32–3 and Cynic teaching. All the items on Cassius' list can be read as purely antinomian in the spirit of Diogenes' famous slogan: 'Deface the coinage'. For all can be seen as primarily critical of existing institutions and conventions of the *polis*. The proposition (2) that only the good are citizens, friends, etc. makes no explicit reference to conventions or institutions. But on Zeno's paradoxical finding, what citizenship, friendship, etc. have in common is that they are all functions of moral goodness (and their opposites of its absence). Reading (a) will take the moral of this to be: don't think about society and the *polis*, think about moral virtue. That is not in itself an antinomian injunction, but the antinomianism of Zeno's other recommendations is a natural consequence of it. For if only moral virtue really matters, the conventions of the *polis* do not; and acquiescence in them may induce the conviction that they do. So acquiescence is to be actively and indeed dramatically discouraged. Little wonder in that case if people joked that the *Republic* was written 'on the dog's tail' (D.L. VII 4). Zeno had, of course, sat at the feet of Diogenes' pupil Crates. On reading (a) the *Republic* teaches an anti-political doctrine entirely consistent with the poem (D.L. VI 85) in which Crates locates the ideal city in the philosopher's knapsack (a metaphor for self-sufficient virtue).

Reading (b) is not in truth very far removed from reading (a). The only point where the two need diverge is over the interpretation of proposition (2): only the good are citizens, friends, kin and free. Reading (b) will not dispute that Zeno here makes citizenship, friendship etc. in some sense functions of moral goodness. But of course it remains unclear whether this is because they are to be analysed and defined in terms of it, or because only the morally good could properly satisfy definitions couched in terms which do not themselves include reference to moral goodness. Either way it is highly unlikely that Zeno will have so revised the concepts of citizenship, friendship etc. as to remove from them any recognizably social or political dimension at all. To work out what it was, and so what his constructive vision of society was, reading (b) looks for guidance elsewhere. One possibility is to exploit a famous passage of Plutarch (*de Alex. virt.* 329 A–B) which alleges that in the *Republic* Zeno advised us 'to regard all men as members of the populace and fellow-citizens'; and to suppose that 'men' means 'good men' or 'sages' (or displaces 'good men' or 'sages' in Zeno's original text). I discuss the dubious value of this text as evidence of the *Republic* in Appendix A. Another possibility – alternatively or additionally – is to consult later Stoic tradition, on the assumption that it is likely to reflect the way the *Republic* was read in the school. One immediately thinks of the famous doctrine, expressed to be sure in various forms, that the universe itself is the only true city (e.g. Clem. *Strom.* IV 26, *SVF* III 327):

> The Stoics say that the universe (οὐρανός) is in the proper sense a city, but that those here on earth are not – they are called cities, but are not really. For a city or a people (δῆμος) is something morally good (σπουδαῖον), an organization or group of men (ἀνθρώπων) administered by law which exhibits refinement (ἀστεῖον).

Reading (b) then brings the doctrine of the true city to bear on proposition (2), and infers that for Zeno the morally good or the wise constitute a community regardless of where in the universe each of them happens to live – just in virtue of being good and wise. It thus succeeds in combining the advantages of a Cynic antinomian reading of most of what D.L. VII 32–3 tells us about the *Republic* with those of a positive, albeit revisionist, interpretation of the notion of community implicit in item (2). Just how or why what the good and wise belong to counts as a community or city would need further explanation. The final two clauses of Clement's report presumably constitute attempts by Chrysippus or his successors to give a precision to the concept of city it did not have in Zeno.

The question that begins to pose itself is: what is the context to which Zeno's *Republic* belongs? Proponents of reading (c) would argue that the right answer comes neither from those contemporaries and successors who were most impressed by its Cynic features nor from later Stoicism, which was no doubt prone to read its own preoccupations into the pithy and sometimes cryptic pronouncements of the founder of the school. Any Greek philosopher who wrote a *Republic* will have been challenging comparison with Plato's great work.[4] Reading (c) will infer that Zeno may therefore be presumed to have been attempting, like Plato, to show how a *polis* – on the ordinary understanding of *polis* – can be reformed or reconstructed to satisfy some cherished goal or goals.

In this chapter I shall argue that reading (c) is the correct one. My argument will make frequent recourse to antecedents of Zeno's ideas in Plato's work, especially the *Republic*. Several of the provisions itemized in D.L. VII 32–3, of course, are naturally interpreted as repeating elements in Plato's communist programme or as pushing it further than Plato himself had done. This is true of the key proposal (3) that women be held in common. Nakedness ((6): presumably in communal gymnastic exercises)[5] is also a notable feature of Plato's arrangements,[6] reinforced by a rule about unisex clothing ((6) again: presumably for everyday, non-gymnastic purposes). Item (5), on the other hand, prohibiting coinage, echoes Plato's actual words only to contradict them: although the divergence is more apparent than real, since the words in question occur in the account of the original city (the 'city of pigs'), whereas the guardians are apparently forbidden to use money.[7] Other comparisons and contrasts are more speculative: for example, the doctrine that only the good are citizens and friends (2) might seem to suggest that Plato's class system is misconceived. This is the sort of point one would expect Zeno to be making if, as seems likely enough, it is in this work that he 'wrote in reply to Plato's *Republic*' (Plu. *Stoic. rep.* 1034 F).

More important than any of these institutional provisions is the purpose for which they are introduced. This is what the chapter will focus on. It will transpire that, as with Plato, so in Zeno the objective is conceived not in terms of the ethics of the individual, but constitutes a specifically political ideal: the same political

[4] Particularly if it was his *first* book, as Zeno's *Republic* is often taken to have been, on the strength of D.L. VII 4 and Philodemus, *On the Stoics*, col. IX. 1–15. But for an excellent treatment of these texts see Erskine, *The Hellenistic Stoa*, pp. 9–15, who shows that their implication that the *Republic* was written in Zeno's youth is so much a function of the sorts of controversies about the work we examined in Ch. 1 as to be worthless as historical evidence.

[5] Cf. Phld. *On the Stoics*, col. XIX. 17–22.

[6] *Rep.* 452 A–B, 457 A–B.

[7] *Rep.* 371 B, 416 E–417 B.

ideal, in fact, as Plato has in view in the *Republic* and elsewhere – friendship and concord, understood in the ordinary senses of those words. Where Zeno differs from Plato is principally in the role he assigns to erotic love in cementing the city together in concord.

II

Two pieces of evidence strongly support the reading (c) of Zeno's *Republic* which takes it to be putting forward a communistic ideal of the same kind as Plato's *Republic* had advocated. The first is a report on the Stoics which amplifies item (3) on Cassius' list (D.L. VII 131):

> Their view is that among the wise, women should be held in common, so that any man at all may have sexual relations with any woman at all, as Zeno says in the *Republic* and Chrysippus in *On Republic* [but also Diogenes the Cynic and Plato].[8] And we shall feel paternal affection for all children alike, and there will be an end to the jealousies arising from adultery.

This text clearly envisages a community whose members are known to one another and live in more or less close proximity to one another.[9] An overriding concern for concord is obvious. How much of what is said is due to Zeno and how much to Chrysippus is impossible to tell. But Chrysippus is in any case likely to have been interpreting Zeno, particularly if *On Republic* was designed as a defence and explanation of Zeno's *Republic*.[10] His authority

[8] Editors often exclude these words, I think rightly. They do not properly continue the *laudatio*, for they contain no reference to book titles. In general the Stoic doxography in D.L. VII seldom refers to the views of non-Stoics on the subjects under discussion: the sole instance is at VII 127 (if we discount this controversial example).

[9] Erskine, *The Hellenistic Stoa*, p. 21, thinks otherwise. But he does not explain what it would mean to rule that women are to be held in common if this is not the case; and the concern about jealousy suggests that even if Zeno did not assume mutual knowledge as a universal feature of his city, he was interested enough in its consequences to devote thought to ways of optimizing them (this is likewise the natural interpretation of his provisions on dress, D.L. VII 33).

[10] *On Republic* apparently contained a statement that Zeno's *Republic* really was by Zeno – or at any rate a reference to the work which was usable as such a statement by those engaged in controversy about it (D.L. VII 34). Other refer-

would give us at least indirect reason to favour reading (c) as the right option to take.

The second passage comes from Book XIII of Athenaeus' *Deipnosophists*. Discussion has turned (561A) to the subject of love (ἔρως). 'Very many philosophical speeches (λόγοι) were given', we are told, including quotations supplied by Athenaeus from Pindar and Euripides, 'the philosopher of the stage'. Then comes a reference to Zeno (561C):

> Pontianus [one of the *dramatis personae*] said that Zeno of Citium took love to be a god who brings about friendship and freedom, and again concord, but nothing else. That is why in the *Republic* he said that Love is a god, there as a helper in furthering the safety of the city.

Writers on Stoic ethics ancient or modern seldom say much about their views on ἔρως, i.e. erotic or passionate love; and the Stoic sage is popularly regarded as doing all he does guided by passionless reason. The starring role in Zeno's *Republic* accorded to love here is therefore unexpected and may strain faith in Athenaeus' credibility. But the information on Zeno put in Pontianus' mouth, like thousands of similar instances in Athenaeus' pages, appears to be in essence, if not in every detail, a decent scrap of doxography. It coheres both with some other items of information relating to views held by Zeno and the early Stoa, and more generally with evidence of considerable interest in erotic love among early Stoic writers. And we should in any case be open to the possibility that Zeno's moral and political theory had an individuality, as well as an affinity with Platonic and Aristotelian

ences to Chrysippus' work make it either simply repeat theses of Zeno's *Republic* (D.L. VII 131: on community of women) or theses of Zeno which may well belong to the *Republic* (D.L. VII 188, Sextus *M* XI 192 = *PH* III 246 [which points out the Zenonian parallel]: on incest), or argue for an explicitly Cynic moral simplicity obviously in the spirit of Zeno's work (Plu. *Stoic. rep.* 1044 B–E: on pleasure and the necessities of life; Phld. *On the Stoics*, col. XV.31–XVI.1: on the uselessness of weapons). *All* these topics are in fact Cynic: which makes it attractive to conjecture that Chrysippus was deliberately reaffirming the Cynic strand or strands in Zeno's *Republic* – although further speculation about what controversial aim he had in doing so is probably profitless. His references to Diogenes were certainly uncompromising: 'He praises Diogenes for masturbating in public and for saying to those present: "Would that I could also rub the hunger out of my belly in this way."' (Plu. *Stoic. rep.* 1044 B).

thought, which may have got ironed out in the systematic development of Stoic philosophy during subsequent generations.

Diogenes Laertius' reports of Stoic literary activity in this area merit attention. The very first Stoics were not for the most part prolific authors by comparison with some of their contemporaries: Epicurus, for example, or Theophrastus and Strato. But all the leading figures among them wrote on erotic love. D.L. VII 33 refers to Zeno's *Art of Love*, and tells us that his *Conversations* contained similar material. Other titles are: Persaeus, *On loves* (VII 36); Ariston, *Erotic conversations* (VII 163); Cleanthes, *On Love* and *Art of Love* (VII 175; but Cleanthes *was* quite prolific); and finally from the rather younger Sphaerus, *Dialogues on Love* (VII 178). There were also at least two works on the subject in Chrysippus' huge corpus: *On Love* (VII 129) and *Letters on Love* (Clem. *Rom. homil.* V 18, *SVF* II 1072). Zeno's first associates are likely to have fastened on the topic because it particularly preoccupied them all, not because orthodoxy required it of them (Ariston for one acknowledged no Zenonian orthodoxy).[11] It is tempting not only to judge that love was indeed as prominent a theme of Zeno's *Republic* as Athenaeus' testimony suggests, but to guess that its prominence in the book was a principal stimulus to a common appetite for the subject in the Stoic school.

III

The Athenaeus text implies that erotic love had a central place in Zeno's conception of the *polis*.[12] In order to understand why, we must consider his fundamental doctrine about love, which was also enunciated in the *Republic* (D.L. VII 129):

> The wise man will love those young persons who by their appearance manifest a natural endowment for virtue, as Zeno says in the *Republic* and Chrysippus in the first book of *On Lives* and Apollodorus in his *Ethics*.

I divide my remarks on this text under four heads.

[11] On this point see A.M. Ioppolo, *Aristone di Chio e lo stoicismo antico* (Rome 1980), with my review 'Ariston of Chios and the unity of virtue', *Ancient Philosophy* 4 (1984) 83–96.

[12] The Stoic theory of love is discussed by D. Babut, 'Les Stoïciens et l'amour', *REG* 76 (1963) 55–63.

(a) Love not a passion

It is to be presumed that Zeno did not think of erotic love as what the Stoics called a passion (πάθος), i.e. – to cite the definition Diogenes Laertius ascribes to him – 'a movement of soul which is irrational and contrary to nature' (D.L. VII 110). If he did, he could hardly have allowed that the sage will love. In fact he probably did not explicitly define love at all. For we find in the sources two different definitions of love ascribed to the Stoics, both of which look as though they are later attempts to give formal articulation to the idea Zeno had in mind in the *Republic*.

One of these [A] is a lucky survivor: it appears just once in the literature, volunteered by Diadumenus' fairly quiet interlocutor in Plutarch's *On Common Conceptions*. It sticks particularly close to what I have called Zeno's fundamental doctrine on love (Plu. *Comm. not.* 1073 B):

> Love is a sort of chase[13] after a youngster (μειρακίου) who is undeveloped but naturally endowed for virtue.

The other, [B], is obviously the official school definition. It exploits not only the fundamental doctrine but the connection between love and friendship attested by Athenaeus, thus incidentally providing further confirmation of the soundness of his evidence. A number of slightly different formulations of [B] are reported. The fullest is in Arius Didymus (Stob. II 115.1–2; cf. e.g. II 66.11–13, D.L. VII 130, Alex. *in Top.* 139.21ff., Schol. in Dion. Thrac. (p. 120.3–5 Hilgard: *SVF* III 721), Cic. *TD* IV 72; alluded to but not cited in Plu. *Comm. not.* 1073 B):

> Love is an attempt[14] to make friends, on account of beauty being apparent, with young persons in bloom.

[13] The idea of love as a chase (θήρα) has Platonic antecedents: see *Lysis* 205 E–206 A, *Symposium* 203 D (cf. *Prot.* 309 A). There is perhaps an echo of definition [A] at Stob. II 108.5–7, where the morally good man is said to be 'given to associating with people, and consequently tactful and given to encouraging and chasing them by means of association with a view to good-will and friendship'.

[14] For this sense of ἐπιβόλη see *LSJ* s.v. 3; Cicero translates its occurrence in [B] as *conatus* (*TD* IV 72). The word ἐπιβόλη is seldom used in texts relating to the old Stoa; no doubt reflection on its employment in [B] prompted the definition of the term recorded in a list of definitions of species of ὁρμή, impulse, at Stob. II 87.18: ὁρμὴ πρὸ ὁρμῆς, 'impulse before impulse'. For an orthodox early Stoic every action or behaviour requires a psychological event: an impulse. So at-

Neither [A] nor [B] concerns itself with the psychology of love. They are both behavioural definitions.[15]

Plutarch, however, implies that the Stoics actually denied that love was a passion. For he takes their view of it to be contrary to ordinary usage and common conceptions. The reason for this is, apparently, precisely that they say it is not a passion, since otherwise the following remark of his has no force (*Comm. not.* 1073 C):

> Nobody would stop the enthusiasm of the wise for the young, given that there is no passion (πάθος) in it, if it is called 'a chase' [cf. [A]] or 'making friends' [cf. [B]] – but they wouldn't let them call it 'love'.[16]

It may have been the author of [B] who was responsible for the denial. One of the texts which preserves his definition introduces it as follows (Stob. II 66.11–13):

> Love is neither desire nor is it for any morally bad thing, but it is an attempt to make friends on account of an appearance of beauty.

In Stoic theory desire (ἐπιθυμία) is one of the four principal species of passion, so to deny that love is desire is tantamount to denying that it is a passion.[17] If the authors of [A] and [B] had been

tempts (which I take to be behaviours) require their own special kind of impulse. 'Impulse before impulse' constitutes a shot at saying what kind that is. It presumably exploits the thought that someone who says to himself: 'Make the attempt to do *X*' is uttering not the simple imperative: 'Do *X*', but a more complex one: 'Bring yourself to do *X*' or 'Do what is necessary in order to do *X*' – prescribing an action which can only be specified in terms of doing *X* but is somehow prior to it. For a recent discussion of ἐπιβόλη on very different lines see B. Inwood, *Ethics and Human Action in Early Stoicism* (Oxford 1985), Appendix 2, esp. pp. 232–3.

15 Thus I take the explanation of ἐπιβόλη as a psychological phenomenon at Stob. II 87.18 (discussed in n. 14 above) to be a Stoic attempt to make out of Zeno's remarks on love a proper psychological definition. That is not what Zeno himself had in mind.

16 Reading ἔρωτα δέ καλεῖν (MSS), and punctuating with a comma after προσαγορευομένην. But the meaning is broadly the same even if we emend as e.g. with Cherniss in the Loeb, or Pohlenz in the Teubner.

17 It is striking, and presumably due ultimately to Zeno's influence, that ἔρως is the only state of mind ordinarily conceived of as a passion or desire (ἐπιθυμία) that is not invariably defined as such in standard Stoic lists of desires. Thus at Stob. II 91.15–16 definition [B] is given; in pseudo-Andronicus περὶ πάθων 4, p. 231.85–91 [B] is one of four definitions of ἔρως – the others are ἐπιθυμία

prepared to venture a positive view about the psychology of ἔρως, they would doubtless have described it as an impulse in accordance with reason: not something purely ratiocinative, but an expression of the whole personality, conceived in good Stoic fashion as a unity. Their silence on the subject presumably reflects the fact that Zeno had not addressed it.

(b) Ethical attractiveness

Like Plato in the *Symposium* and *Phaedrus*, Zeno marries responsiveness to the physical attractions of adolescents with high ethical purpose. The marriage as contrived by Zeno is theoretically more satisfying – or at any rate it evades a difficulty in Plato's position. On Plato's premisses, there is no reason why someone who exhibits the physical beauty which provokes the philosopher's desire must also be someone likely to develop into a morally admirable person. This might be called the 'Alcibiades problem'. Stoic materialism, however, took states of character to be bodies, and as bodies perceptible. The pithiest formulation of the idea comes in an entertaining anecdote about how Cleanthes was able to spot a passive homosexual by his sneeze, thus successfully defending the Zenonian thesis that 'character can be known from appearance (εἶδος)' (D.L. VII 173). Plutarch evidently takes the idea to be relevant to discussion of the Stoics' teaching on love, because he refers to it in *Comm. not.* ch. 28 when he reports them as saying that depravity of character infects the appearance (εἶδος) (Plu. *Comm. not.* 1073 B). The perceptibility of character affords

σωματικῆς συνουσίας, desire for bodily intercourse, ἐπιθυμία φιλῶν, desire for friendship, and ὑπηρεσία θεῶν εἰς νέων κατακόσμησιν καὶ καλῶν, service of the gods directed to the ordering of young and beautiful persons. The first two appear to be Peripatetic (cf. D.L. V 31, Stob. II 142.24, and especially Hermias *in Plat. Phdr.* p. 34.4 Couvreur); the third seems to derive from Polemo (Plu. *ad princ. inerud.* 780 D). For discussion see A. Glibert-Thirry; *Pseudo-Andronicus de Rhodes 'ΠΕΡΙ ΠΑΘΩΝ'* (Leiden 1977), p. 28 and n. 93, and p. 34; the parallel texts are reproduced on p. 292. D.L. VII 113 on love is evidently lacunose. All the other definitions in this paragraph specify an elaborately qualified form of ἐπιθυμία. The account of love reads: 'Love is a sort of desire', but without further qualification. The text presumably breaks off here; when it resumes it is obviously describing another sort of love, namely that which characterizes the morally good. For it runs: '... not in the case of the morally good: for it is an attempt to make friends on account of beauty being apparent' – i.e. [B] once again.

Zeno a solution to the 'Alcibiades problem', which is suggested by the formulation of the fundamental doctrine on love recorded in Diogenes Laertius (VII 129). There is a specifically ethical form of attractiveness in an adolescent which will appeal to the wise man, i.e. that characteristic of natural endowment for virtue: 'by their appearance (εἶδος) they manifest a natural endowment for virtue'.[18] This was presumably lacking in Alcibiades – although Plutarch argued to the contrary, on the ground precisely that Socrates loved him (*Alcib.* 4, 1).

(c) Educational purpose

What does the wise man hope to effect by his pursuit of the beloved? He will want to help him to mature from endowment for virtue to virtue itself. Or so it would be natural to expect, particularly in view of the Platonic precedent, e.g. *Symp.* 209 B–C:

> So he welcomes beautiful bodies in preference to ugly ones, seeing that he is pregnant. And if he encounters a soul that is beautiful and noble and naturally endowed (εὐφυεῖ), he gives an emphatic welcome to the combination of the two. In relation to this person he is at once well supplied with arguments about virtue and regarding the sort of person the good man should be and what pursuits he should engage in, and he tries to educate him.

Two texts do something to confirm the expectation. First is a textually corrupt passage in Stobaeus, which supplies a Stoic definition of the science of love (II 66.6–8):

> It is knowledge of the chase after naturally endowed young people, [a knowledge] which is directed towards turning them to living in accordance with virtue.

[18] For further discussion of the definitions these words of Zeno inspired see Appendix B. For observations on the role of εὐφυΐα, 'natural endowment [for virtue]', in early Stoic ethics see A.M. Ioppolo, *Aristone di Chio*, pp. 120–3. A political application of the idea is reported by Arius Didymus: 'The man who has sense will one day be king, and he will live with a king who manifests both natural endowment and the desire to learn' (Stob. II 111.3–5: note the repetition of the phrase ἐμφαίνειν εὐφυΐαν). There is more discussion of ethical attractiveness in Appendix C.

'Directed towards turning' corresponds to a rather insecure reading in the Greek text;[19] and to get it to say 'to living in accordance with virtue' an emendation is necessary[20] (although it is obvious that this is the sense required). If these problems may be set aside, it transpires that the erotic chase spoken of in [A] has a missionary aim: care and indeed conversion of the soul. An educational purpose likewise emerges from a further passage of Athenaeus (563 E):

> You [sc. the Stoics] are oglers of boys, and in this alone emulate the founder of your philosophy Zeno the Phoenician, who never consorted with a woman, but always with boy-friends, as Antigonus of Carystus records in his *Life* of him. For you are always repeating that it is necessary to love not bodies but soul: you who say that we should keep on with those we are in love with until they are 28 years old.

Admittedly this quotation, like the definition of the science of love, talks about the Stoics in general, not Zeno. But the highly specific recommendation that the erotic relationship should be kept on until the ἐρώμενος, the boy-friend, is 28, once more points to the *Republic*. Not only does it fit with Zeno's stress on the sage's attention to ethical promise: moral maturation takes longer than physical, so the Stoic ἐρώμενος remains an ἐρώμενος well into the time of life at which his non-Stoic contemporary would have graduated to the role of ἐράστης. The numerical precision is reminiscent of nothing so much as the rules Plato and Aristotle, in their political writings, lay down in their *educational* legislation.[21]

[19] I opt tentatively for πρός τρέψιν P; Wachsmuth emends to προτρεπτικήν. The gist is the same. For protreptic to virtue and philosophy as a characteristic activity of the sage see Stob. II 104.10–105.6.

[20] The MSS have ἐπὶ τὴν κατ' ἀρετήν, printed by Wachsmuth. His note in the *app. crit.* suggests ἐπὶ τὰ κατ' ἀρετήν, which seems on the right lines.

[21] Cf. Pl. *Rep.* 537 A–540 A; Ar. *Pol.* 1335 b26ff., 1336 b35ff., who follows 'those who divide life into periods of seven years'. There is other evidence besides Athen. 563 E that the Stoics also adhered to a scheme of seven-year periods: the notorious conflict in the sources over whether they thought reason was complete at age 7 (Aët. IV 11, 4 = *SVF* II 83) or the more plentifully and convincingly attested 14 (Aët. V 23, 1 = *SVF* II 764; Schol. ad Plat. Alcib. I, p. 121 E and Stob. I 317, 21 = *SVF* I 149). Marrou (*Histoire de l'Education dans l'Antiquité* (Paris 1965, 6th ed.), p. 161), writes as follows: 'Hippocrate, nous dit-on, partageait la vie humaine en huit périodes de sept ans: l'éducation classique réclamait pour elle les trois premières, que désignent les noms de

Where else in mainstream Stoic literature than in Zeno's *Republic* would one expect to find a similar legislative provision?

(d) *Making friends*

Zeno's *Republic*, if we may believe Athenaeus (561 C, cited in Section II), represented friendship at least as a consequence of love. Whether interpreting Zeno or not, Chrysippus made friendship its actual object; and it is this view which is incorporated into [B] (D.L. VII 130):

> Love is an attempt to make friends, on account of beauty being apparent: its object is not sexual intercourse, but friendship. At all events, Thrasonides, although he had the woman he loved in his power, abstained from intercourse with her because she hated him. So love has friendship as its object, as in fact Chrysippus says in *On Love*, and it is not a matter for censure.

A lover often hopes that, if his beloved reciprocates his affection, the two of them will be friends, and indeed achieve a friendship special in quality. Plato's *Lysis* is striking testimony that ancient Greek lovers entertained the same hope.[22] But there was presumably a particular ethical twist to this story as told by Zeno or Chrysippus. Only good or wise men can be friends; the object of a wise man's love is someone naturally endowed for virtue, but not yet virtuous. It seems to follow that love in a sense aims to transcend itself. If the lover succeeds in helping his beloved mature into virtue, it is then no longer love but friendship which is an appropriate relationship with him. Friendship consummates love – and replaces it.[23]

παιδίον, "petit enfant" (au-dessous de sept ans), παῖς, "enfant" (de sept à quatorze ans), et μειράκιον, "adolescent" (de quatorze à vingt et un).' For discussion of a vast amount of pertinent evidence see J. Mansfeld, *The Pseudo-Hippocratic Tract ΠΕΡΙ ΕΒΔΟΜΑΔΩΝ Ch. 1–11 and Greek Philosophy* (Assen 1971), especially pp. 168–178; cf. also a useful summary treatment in R. Garland, *The Greek Way of Life* (London 1990), Introduction. What the Stoic view reported by Athenaeus effectively says is: education needs to go on another seven years beyond the first three periods accepted by e.g. Aristotle.

[22] For further evidence of this in Plato and Xenophon see Dover, *Greek Homosexuality* (London 1978), p. 53.

[23] It appears that Diogenes of Babylon actually spoke of friendship as the τέλος, goal or fulfilment, of love: Phld. *Mus.* p. 17.11–15; cf. p. 84.35–40.

Which is more fundamental? The disinterested concern that my beloved achieve virtue (cf. (c) above)? Or the pursuit of him, in the attempt to get him to be my friend? The authors of definitions [A] and [B] in effect take the second option. Rightly so. My concern is not the impartial desire that those with the right make-up for virtue should realize their promise, still less the impersonal wish that virtue should be achieved where there is the potentiality for it. It is *my* beloved I want to achieve virtue, because he is or could be in a particular relationship with *me*: which is not incompatible with wanting it for *his* sake, not mine.[24]

IV

Zeno's view that Love is a god who contributes to the safety of the city cries out for demythologization. In the light of the evidence about his teaching on love reviewed in Section III, we might reformulate it as the thesis that erotic love promotes the security of the communist state whose institutions are referred to at D.L. VII 32–3. Does this thesis have anything to recommend it as a piece of socio-political analysis? Certainly there are grounds for a positive answer if we consider the ancient Greek phenomenon of homosexual love.

We are not here concerned with homosexuality as a stable and often exclusive sexual orientation, with deep roots in the psychology of the individual. What Zeno presumably had in mind was the kind of acculturated homosexual behaviour among the ancient Greeks in which particularly upper-class young males, both adult and adolescent, quite generally engaged for a limited period of their lives, before graduating to marriage and fatherhood. It is what George Devereux calls pseudo-homosexuality.[25] Its classic representatives are Achilles and Patroclus in myth, and Harmodius and Aristogeiton in history. The excitable romantic atmo-

[24] Disinterestedness in friendship is insisted on by the Stoics (D.L. VII 124): 'They say that friendship exists only among the morally good, on account of their likeness; and they say that it is a kind of sharing in the affairs of life, in which we treat our friends as we do ourselves.' On the Stoic conception of friendship see further J.-C. Fraisse, *Philia. La notion d'amitié dans la philosophie antique* (Paris 1974) 348–73.

[25] G. Devereux, 'Greek pseudo-homosexuality and the "Greek miracle"', *Symb. Osl.* 42 (1967) 69–92.

sphere of the gymnasia in which it flourished in classical Athens (or at any rate the Athens of his imagination) is memorably depicted in Plato's dialogues.

Ancient Greek homosexuality has been much discussed in recent years from many points of view. But there is one observation made in one way or another by various authors which seems fundamental. I quote the formulation in Dover's study *Greek Homosexuality*:[26]

> The Greek city-state was continuously confronted with the problem of survival in competition with aggressive neighbours, and for this reason the fighter, the adult male citizen, was the person who mattered. The power to deliberate and take political decisions and the authority to approve or disapprove of social and cultural innovation were strongly vested in the adult male citizens of the community; the inadequacy of women as fighters promoted a general devaluation of the intellectual capacity and emotional stability of women; and the young male was judged by such indication as he afforded of his worth as a potential fighter. Sparta and Crete alone went to the length of constructing a society in which familial and individual relationships were both formally and effectively subordinated to military organization; elsewhere varied and fluctuating degrees of compromise between the claims of community, family and individual prevailed. Males tended to group themselves together for military, political, religious and social purposes to a degree which fell short of welding them into a totally efficient fighting-machine but was nevertheless enough to inhibit the full development of intimacy between husband and wife or between father and son.

The organization of Sparta and Crete on a military model is especially pertinent to our concerns. A society organized as a fighting-machine will necessarily give the family a reduced role and status, and thereby diminish the value and significance of the vertical relationships of parent and child, young and old, as well as the importance of marriage. By the same token the horizontal or near-horizontal relationship between male adolescent

[26] Dover, *Greek Homosexuality*, pp. 201–2.

and young unmarried adult male is bound to grow in importance and intensity. Society will encourage and exploit it. It is to be expected that in this context homosexuality will flourish: it is highly functional.

That it did flourish at Sparta and in Crete seems clear from the evidence, which is admittedly scrappy and already distorted by moralizing preoccupations or other prejudices.[27] Plato had plenty of reason to want to think the best of Crete and Sparta. Notoriously he disapproves of the way that in these states the organization of common meals and gymnastic exercises has led, as he believes, to the perversions, as he sees it, of homosexual intercourse (*Laws* 636 AB, 836 BC). Aristotle agrees that homosexuality is prevalent among the Cretans (*Pol.* 1272a23–6), but portrays the Spartans as weakened rather by compulsive attraction to their women (1269b12–70a11). However this seems to be a fallacious inference from the power of women in Spartan society.[28] The most remarkable text relating to Crete is a passage of Strabo (10.4.20–1) reproducing an account in Ephorus (mid-fourth century) of ritualized homosexual rape of a boy by his ἐραστής. For Sparta we have not only general accounts of laws and customs but the detail of political and military history, on which Anton Powell comments that 'references to particular homosexual attachments of Spartans are conspicuous even by Greek standards'.[29] For example:

> We read... in Xenophon's *Hellenika* of a Spartan commander, Anaxibios, who found himself in a hopeless military position and chose, with fellow officers, to stand his ground and die. The rest of the force fled, save for Anaxibios' παιδικά, who stayed by his side, evidently until death. Xenophon's point in referring to this devoted individual by his sexual status, and not by his name, is probably that the sexuality [sc. of the relationship] produced the exceptional loyalty.

[27] Cf. Dover, *Greek Homosexuality*, Ch. IV, Section A.

[28] On which see e.g. P.A. Cartledge, 'Spartan wives: liberation or licence?', *CQ* 31 (1981) 84–105; A.S. Bradford, 'Gynaikokratoumenoi: did Spartan women rule Spartan men?', *Ancient World* 14 (1986) 13 ff.; S. Hodkinson, 'Inheritance, marriage and demography: perspectives upon the success and decline of classical Sparta', in *Classical Sparta: Techniques behind her Success*, ed. A. Powell (London 1989), Ch. 4.

[29] A. Powell, *Athens and Sparta* (London 1988), p. 225.

Powell's interpretation is supported by a passage in Xenophon's *Symposium* (8.35) which claims that Spartan ἐρασταί make their ἐρώμενοι so virtuous that even if stationed in the battle-line with strangers apart from their lovers they are just as ashamed to desert their comrades-in-arms.

From our point of view two pieces of information in Plutarch's *Lycurgus* are particularly interesting. First, he makes paederasty part of the ἀγωγή, the fearsome education system compulsory for all Spartan boys (*Lyc.* 17–18). One notable provision of the ἀγωγή (as also in Crete) was that authority over an adolescent was transferred from the father to the community, and responsibility for his further upbringing was then vested by it in specially appointed officials. It appears that he would normally acquire an ἐραστής and that the ἐραστής would gain kudos, or lose face if his ἐρώμενος did poorly in tests of virtue and intelligence. The ἐραστής will presumably have served as a role-model for the ἐρώμενος, although whether the evidence is sufficient to support the idea that he could be regarded as engaged in educating or training him, or in displaced fathering, seems more moot. Cartledge[30] (who with Dover and Devereux thinks he could) is certainly persuasive in his suggestion that the friendship of an older (but not much older) person, himself a full member of the citizen-body, would have provided the adolescent with a way of coping with the colossal stress of the Spartan system, and with the ambivalence about other human beings, especially adults, which it must have induced.

The other Plutarch text deserving attention is really only a single sentence (*Lyc.* 25.1):

> Men under the age of thirty absolutely never went to market, but had the transactions necessary for the management of their households carried out for them by means of their kinsmen and ἐρασταί.

It is hard to know what to make of this. The impression left by the ancient evidence on homosexuality in general, not contradicted by the Spartan material, is that ἐρασταί themselves were normally

[30] Paul Cartledge, 'The politics of Spartan pederasty', *PCPS* 207 (1981) 17–36, at p. 28. Cf. n. 33 below.

unmarried young men of between twenty and thirty.[31] Hodkinson offers the plausible suggestion that the restriction reported by Plutarch was a survival 'from an earlier period when men were not permitted to marry until thirty when they finally left the ἀγωγή and became fully adult'.[32] There could be an obvious military rationale for forbidding marriage before thirty, and for encouraging ἐραστής and ἐρώμενος to maintain their relationship until the younger of them reached that age. Here we are in the realm of speculation – but fascinatingly close to the Stoic injunction to continue with one's ἐρώμενος until he is twenty-eight.

There can be no reasonable doubt, then, that homosexuality was a key ingredient of the Spartan social system. Its rationale, as I have argued, is presumably to be seen in its contribution to the cohesiveness of the male club which was Sparta. Some of its features, notably the two we have identified in Plutarch's *Lycurgus*, are parallel to ideas about love which were presented, if I am right, in Zeno's *Republic*. Indeed, in the hands of the moralists Sparta becomes even more like Zeno's city. Here is Xenophon (*Lac. Pol.* 2.13–14):

> If someone, who was himself what a person should be, admired a boy's soul, and tried to make of him a friend without reproach and to associate with him, he [sc. Lycurgus] would approve and think this to be education of the finest sort. But if someone was clearly desiring a boy's body, he ruled that this was very shameful, and made lovers in Sparta abstain from their boy-friends no less than parents abstain from sex with their children and brothers from brothers. But I am not surprised some do not believe this. For in many cities the laws do not oppose lust for boys.

Although the ἐραστής–ἐρώμενος relationship appears to have had its place within the context of the ἀγωγή, Xenophon's treatment of homosexual love as itself παιδεία (education) is doubtless an unconvincing exercise in idealization – Platonization, in fact. If the name of Zeno were substituted for Lycurgus the passage

[31] So Dover, *Greek Homosexuality*, p. 171; F. Buffière, *Eros adolescent* (Paris 1980), pp. 605–17.

[32] Hodkinson, 'Inheritance, Marriage and Demography', in Powell (ed.), *Classical Sparta*, p. 109.

would constitute an excellent paraphrase of his teaching in the *Republic*.[33]

Indeed, the Spartan constitution as described by writers like Critias, Xenophon and Dicaearchus was very likely one of the models Zeno followed in working out the proposals of the *Republic*, as of course it was for Plato too in his *Republic*. For what it is worth, Plutarch probably actually tells us as much (*Lyc.* 31.1–3):

> It was not this that was Lycurgus' main achievement, to leave the city exercising leadership over a great number of other cities. Rather, he thought that, as in the life of a single man, so happiness for a whole city comes into being from virtue and concord with itself. So he ordered it and brought it into harmony with this in view, that having achieved a liberal and self-sufficient form of life they might continue in it for a very long time by practising self-restraint. This is what Plato too took as the principle of his constitution [or, of the *Republic*], and Diogenes and Zeno and all those who have tried to say something on these matters and win approval for doing so, even though they have left only writings and theories. But he brought into the light not writings and theories, but a constitution not copied [or, inimitable] and achieved in practice. And to those who take the view that the disposition which is said to belong to the wise man is something that could not really exist, he has given a demonstration of a whole city philosophizing. It is therefore no surprise that his reputation exceeds all those who have ever practised politics among the Greeks.

Strictly speaking this passage says only that the philosophers worked out their schemes on the same principle as Lycurgus did,

[33] On the 'consistent Greek tendency to regard homosexual love as a compound of an educational with a genital relationship' (Dover, *Greek Homosexuality*, p. 202) see e.g. Marrou, *Histoire de l'Éducation*, Pt. I Ch. III ('De la pédérastie comme éducation'). 'I will give you good advice, like a father to his son' says Theognis 1049–50; and according to Plutarch the ἐραστής rules the μειράκιον (adolescent) as the nurse does the infant, the teacher the boy, and the law and his general the man who has come of age (*Amatorius* 754 D). Some scholars have gone further, interpreting classical Greek homosexuality as a *rite de passage* by which boys graduated into the adult male warrior-community. There is a good sceptical discussion of this hypothesis in K.J. Dover, *The Greeks and their Legacy* (Oxford 1988), Ch. 12 ('Greek Homosexuality and Initiation').

not that they borrowed it from him.[34] But when Plutarch says that Lycurgus' constitution was ἀμίμητον, he probably means that it was not a copy of someone else's – like Plato's and the rest. In any case there is other evidence that Zeno had the Spartan system in mind.

First, we know that Zeno's close associate Persaeus of Citium wrote a *Spartan Constitution*, as well as a critique of Plato's *Laws* in seven books (D.L. VII 36). It is tempting to infer that this reflects a wish on Zeno's part to distance his political theorizing from Plato's while stressing the Spartan connection. We have no information about the content of Persaeus' attack on the *Laws*, in which there is much that is incompatible with what we know of Zeno's *Republic*: e.g. – to take just one example – emphatic provision for law courts (766 D) and temples (778 BC). But Plato begins with a discussion of the Spartan and Cretan constitutions (624 A ff.); and he singles out for particular criticism their encouragement of homosexuality (636 A–D) and their prohibition on the drinking of wine (636 E ff.). Given what we know of Zeno's position, and in view of the sensitivity of the issue and the prominence Plato accords it, it is hard to conceive that Persaeus' reply did not include a defence of homosexual love and by the same token of Spartan practice. We also know that Zeno and his pupils had things to say about the drinking of wine. The question whether the wise man will get drunk was apparently a standard topic of discussion among the early Stoics, for reasons that are unknown.[35] Perhaps Persaeus' preoccupation with the *Laws* supplies a clue.

[34] So e.g. P. Merlan, 'Alexander the Great or Antiphon the Sophist?', *CP* 45 (1950) 161–6, at pp. 161–2, and H. C. Baldry, 'Zeno's ideal state', *JHS* 79 (1959) 3–15, at p. 8, rejecting the interpretation of W.W. Tarn, *Alexander the Great* (Cambridge 1948), Vol. II p.418. Merlan makes a great deal of the point that τῆς πολιτείας (rendered 'constitution [or *Republic*]' above) means 'constitution', not '*Republic*'. How does he know? Even if his view is correct, Plutarch is obviously *thinking* of the books called *Republic* written by Plato, Zeno and Diogenes. A further objection by Merlan misfires equally badly. 'If Sparta was the basis for Zeno's *Politeia* [as Tarn held], how can Tarn explain that in it Zeno defended (or advocated) promiscuity? In Lycurgus' Sparta the institution of marriage was highly respected.' But obviously Zeno could have admired the communism and homosexual ethos of Spartan life, while also thinking that the Spartans, in maintaining the institution of marriage, did not go far enough in that direction. These is a good general introduction to the question of Zeno's interest in Sparta in E.N. Tigerstedt, *The Legend of Sparta in Classical Antiquity II* (Uppsala 1974) pp. 41–8 (with notes at pp. 317–27).

[35] For some discussion see my paper 'The syllogisms of Zeno of Citium', *Phronesis* 23 (1983) 31–58, at pp. 41–3.

The issue might have been conceived of by the Stoics as a problem put on the agenda of political philosophy by Plato in the *Laws*. If so, Persaeus' critique too would doubtless have engaged with the question. The more junior Sphaerus is credited (D.L. VII 178) with *On Lycurgus and Socrates*, in three books, and *On the Spartan Constitution*, in at least three books (we have a quotation from the third).[36] Sphaerus' interest in the subject was probably more complex than Persaeus'. His Stoic (or, as I am arguing, Zenonian) enthusiasm for Sparta will have found expression of some sort in his role as adviser to Cleomenes III, and was perhaps shaped in part by his experience in the job. For what it is worth, again Plutarch tells us that he assisted Cleomenes in the reintroduction and reform of the ἀγωγή (Plu. *Cleom.* 11; cf. 2).[37]

Second, while most of the institutional proposals in Zeno's *Republic* known to us were probably inspired mostly by reflection on Plato's *Republic* or by conversation with Crates, the Spartan model might well have reinforced his objection to the standard Greek educational system (item (1) on Cassius' list), and provides the only obvious antecedent for his teaching on the importance of love in the education of the young, at any rate insofar as this is seen as contributing to the cohesion of the state.

The greater the similarity between Zeno's city and an idealized Sparta, the more obvious the rationale of the ἐραστής–ἐρώμενος relationship in it; i.e. if Zeno envisages not merely a communist state designed to achieve maximum concord among its citizens, but a state organized as though it were a male club, we can explain the elevation of Love to the status of a deity protecting the security of the city in the same terms as Dover employs to account for homosexuality at Sparta.

[36] Athenaeus IV 141 CD: information about the ἐπάικλα, i.e. after-dinner savouries at the common meal, also the subject of quotations from Persaeus' *Spartan Constitution* (140 EF) and Dicaearchus' *Tripoliticus* (141 A–C). The *Tripoliticus* (cf. Cic. *ad Att.* XIII 32 = fr. 70 W.) is often taken to be the same work as the *Constitution of the Spartiates* ascribed to him in the Suda s.v. (=fr. 1 W.). For further discussion see Elizabeth Rawson, *The Spartan Tradition in European Thought* (Oxford 1969), pp. 82–3.

[37] Sphaerus has sometimes been supposed to have exercised a much more extensive influence on the Spartan revolution than Plutarch explicitly attests: implausibly, in my view (cf. Tigerstedt, *The Legend of Sparta II* pp. 68–70). For a contrary opinion see the recent review of the evidence, with good bibliography, in Erskine, *The Hellenistic Stoa*, Ch. 6.

V

So was Zeno's city a male club? Were women treated as second-class citizens? We know that Zeno's *Republic* like Plato's advocated that (i) women be held in common. But we have no explicit information as to whether Zeno like Plato proposed that (ii) they qualify for the same political responsibilities as men. It is easy to make the mistake of assuming that assent to (i) must go hand in hand with assent to (ii). But Plato argues the two points quite separately in *Rep.* V, on distinct grounds. (i) is based on consideration of what is required if the guardians are to live as harmonious a life as possible, (ii) on an examination of the natural capacities of the two sexes. So we cannot infer Zeno's commitment to (ii) from his allegiance to (i). Is there any other evidence which might enable us to determine his attitude to (ii)?

Stoic ethics is deeply concerned with *human* nature, and particularly with the rationality all humans have in common. We nowhere find the sort of differentiation between male and female capacities made by Aristotle. There is even some reason to think that the school explicitly rejected Aristotle's position, which makes women and slaves naturally inferior kinds of human being. According to Lactantius the Stoics ruled that slaves and women should philosophize; and he plausibly suggests that this was because they saw no difference between their capacities for wisdom and those of men (*Inst.* III 25; cf. also Musonius Rufus *ap.* Stob. II 235.23–239.29, 244.6–247.2). The suggestion receives support from a book title of Cleanthes: *On the thesis that the same virtue belongs to both a man and a woman* (D.L. VII 175), and from evidence that Chrysippus subscribed to the thesis (Phld. *de piet.* col. V 8–11; cf. Antisthenes, D.L. VI 12). Moreover, Zeno's *Republic* abolishes distinctions in dress between men and women, presumably because he holds that there is no fundamental difference in nature between them. He surely has no *reason*, therefore, for discriminating with respect to the functions of citizenship between morally good men and morally good women. We should conclude that he *is* committed to (ii).

Yet if this is Zeno's considered position, it is hard not to suspect sexism and false consciousness at work in his doctrine about the love of the wise for young persons and its role in preserving the city. Is it not probable that when he talks of love he means love by *men* for adolescent *males*? Do not the Platonic and Spartan resonances of his teaching make this the likeliest interpretation? Has Zeno not forgotten – at least temporarily – that women can be sages and so citizens too?[38]

Unfortunately the evidence is insufficient for a decisive answer to these questions. Nonetheless there are one or two considerations which support the view (albeit indirectly) that Zenonian love is a chase after morally promising girls – as well as boys.

First is the precedent of Plato's *Republic*. Plato's guardians include women as well as men; and therefore homosexual love could not for him have the same dynamic unifying function it may rationally assume in an essentially male community like Sparta. What binds Plato's city (or its governors) together is not, as with Zeno, love, but a general sympathy and a universal sense of kinship between young and old, male and female (462 A–465 E). This is what one might call a heterosexual rethinking of the Greek conception of *Kriegskameradschaft*. Plato does follow Greek tradition in associating love with spirit on the battle-field, but no doubt because his community of guardians is a mixed society he adapts the tradition by encouraging love of *either* sex (468 B–C). Here is remarkable testimony to the penetration and tenacity of Plato's political insight, given the intensity of his descriptions of the ἐραστής–ἐρώμενος relationship in the *Symposium* and *Phaedrus*, and the high intellectual, moral and aesthetic claims he makes for it.

Second, we have good reason to believe that in his *Republic* Zeno discussed the physical intercrural intercourse (διαμηρισμός) distinctive of homosexual relationships (Phld. *On the Stoics*, col. XV. 1–9; Plu. *quaest. conv.* 653 E). Sextus preserves fragments of what he wrote on the subject, whether from the *Republic* or elsewhere (cf. D.L. VII 34, which makes *Art of Love* or *Conversations* alternative possibilities). Zeno evidently ruled that like all sexual intercourse it is indifferent for virtue and happiness (cf. Sextus *PH* I 160, III 200; Origen *Contra Celsum* IV 45), and that consequently

[38] For discussion of this kind of false consciousness in earlier Greek political philosophy see my 'Ideology and Philosophy in Aristotle's Theory of Slavery', in G. Patzig (ed.), *Aristotles "Politik"* (Göttingen 1990).

(*M* XI 190 = *PH* III 245):

> Do not have intercourse with the youngster you love in preference to the one you don't (or *vice versa*), or with a female in preference to a male (or *vice versa*). For it is not the case that one thing suits and is suitable for the one you do, another for the one you don't, or one thing for females, another for males, but rather just the same.

What this text shows is that in thinking about love and homosexuality Zeno (1) was alert to the need to consider relations with young women as well as with young men, and (2) found no reason to treat the two sexes differently in *one* important matter (admittedly not Zenonian love proper).[39]

On balance, therefore, we must conclude that Zeno's city was no more a male club than was Plato's.

Yet an interesting contrast with Plato suggests itself. I have argued that because Plato makes guardians of women as well as men, he makes the bond which ties them together not homosexual love (as in Sparta), but the sympathy and mutual commitment characteristic of the family. Perhaps Zeno thought this was a

[39] The material on διαμηρισμός is Cynic in tone (although cf. Plato *Phdr.* 230 E–234 C): which suggests a further consideration in favour of the view that Zeno's treatment of love was not exclusively homosexual in orientation. For Zeno was a pupil of Crates (D.L. VI 105, VII 2–4, etc., confirmed by the existence of a work entitled *Recollections of Crates* in the catalogue of his books (VII 4); a story about Crates is also recorded in Zeno's *Anecdotes* (Χρεῖαι, VI 91–2)). And the love of Hipparchia for Crates, his *logoi* and his way of life, was such as to achieve recognition in Diogenes Laertius' *Life* of Crates (VI 96; cf. Epictet. *Diss.* III 22, 76). She was notorious for wearing the same clothing as her husband and indeed for living the same life-style (VI 93, 97–8). The evidence is all anecdotal, but there is plenty of it (see G. Giannantoni, *Socraticorum Reliquiae* (Naples 1983) II 712–15 [= V H 19–26]) and it presumably constitutes a case of 'no smoke without fire'. It seems not unlikely that the Cynic marriage of Crates and Hipparchia will have done something to shape Zeno's conception of love. There is one text (Clem. *Paidag.* III 11, 74) which appears to describe a sort of person the sage might appropriately love – and it is a male type (see Appendix C). But we cannot infer from it that Zeno believed *only* males were suitable. Again, a fragmentary poem by the third-century Cynic Cercidas firmly associates ἔρως Ζανωνικός, 'Zenonian love', with an apparently sublimated form of male homosexuality: τοῦ[τ'ἔ]στὶ ποτ' ἄρσενας ἄρση[ν, τοῦ]τ' ἔρως Ζανωνικός, P. Oxy 1082 Fr. 4.13–14 (latest edition with commentary by E. Livrea, *Studi Cercidei* (Bonn 1986) 140–58). But while this may give a fair reflection of the impression early Stoic theory and practice made on people, it cannot be taken as a full and accurate summary of doctrine.

wrong turning on Plato's part: the intensity of love – of course a sublimated Platonic form of love – must remain the cement of society; but let it be heterosexual as well as homosexual. In which case Zeno's city will have retained the advantages of the male club without its philosophically unjustifiable restriction to males.

VI

Athenaeus claimed that according to Zeno love brings about friendship, freedom and concord. Examination of other evidence has enabled us to elucidate the meaning of the thesis about love and friendship, confirming its presence and establishing its role in the *Republic*. What of freedom and concord?

There is good reason to think that what Athenaeus says about concord certainly reflects something put forward in the *Republic*. Anxiety about στάσις in Athens at the end of the Peloponnesian War seems to have been the catalyst which made of ὁμόνοια, concord, a key word in the vocabulary of politics and political philosophy, employed initially and fundamentally to formulate a precondition of the internal stability of the state.[40] This is the way it is used in Book IV of Plato's *Republic*, where ὁμόνοια is identified with σωφροσύνη, i.e. with one of the cardinal excellences the ideal state must exemplify, and where indeed the class system central to Plato's theory is so devised as to create the optimal conditions for the emergence of ὁμόνοια (*Rep.* 431 D–432 A). It would accordingly be no surprise to find it taking centre stage in Zeno's political philosophy as well, given that his *Republic* inherits so much from Plato's.

From antecedent probability we turn to the indirect evidence of Arius Didymus' account of Stoic ethics.[41] He implies that

[40] For the evidence and an excellent discussion of it see J. de Romilly, 'Vocabulaire et propagande ou les premiers emplois du mot ὁμόνοια', in *Mélanges de Linguistique et de Philologie Grecques offerts à Pierre Chantraine* (Paris 1972), pp. 199–209.

[41] There is further indirect evidence in the fact that *Chrysippus*' treatise *On Concord* was evidently a political work – at any rate to the same extent as Zeno's *Republic* was political. For it clearly contained different definitions of 'free' and 'slave' (key terms in Zeno's *Republic*, of course: D.L. VII 32–3): see Athenaeus 267 B, with D.L. VII 121. The definitions are the subject of an interesting if speculative treatment in Erskine, *The Hellenistic Stoa*, Ch. 2. Chrysippus' treatise very likely attempted *inter alia* to explain what Zeno meant

the Stoics defined friendship in terms of concord. At Stob. II 106.12–17 the following argument is recorded:

> Moreover they hold the view that every fool is also at enmity with the gods. For enmity is lack of harmony with regard to the affairs of life and discord, just as friendship is harmony and concord. But the morally bad are in disharmony with the gods with regard to the affairs of life. So every fool is at enmity with the gods.

Stob. II 108.15–18 transmits a thesis about friendship which clearly derives ultimately from Zeno's *Republic*, and supports it with an argument which relies on the same definitional equivalence:

> They leave friendship something found among only the wise. For only among these is concord about the affairs of life to be found. Concord is knowledge of common goods.

The notion of concord being employed here was elucidated at the very beginning of Arius Didymus' section on the wise and the foolish (Stob. II 93.19–94.6):

> They say that all good things are common to the morally good, inasmuch as the person who benefits one of his neighbours also benefits himself. Concord is knowledge of common goods, which is why all the morally good are in concord with each other – because they are in harmony in the affairs of life. But the morally bad, being in disharmony with one another, are enemies and given to doing ill to one another and foes.

In what sense is concord knowledge of common goods? The Stoics presumably have in mind the knowledge shared by the wise that goods (i.e. in Stoic theory virtues and virtuous actions) benefit all the wise and morally good, or at any rate all of those who are neighbours. If you and I know that any good benefits both of us, we are evidently at one both in the fact of our intellectual agreement and more importantly in our recognition of the equality between us – viz. that each of us is in as advantageous a position

by such concepts as freedom and concord in the *Republic*. He discussed the related concept of kingship in a work entitled: *On Zeno's having used words in the underivative sense* (κυρίως), according to D.L. VII 122.

as the other with respect to virtuous actions. The connection with harmony is not as crystal clear as it might be. But in an earlier passage Arius Didymus informs us that the Stoics define harmony as 'shared belief about the affairs of life' (Stob. II 74.4–5). When such shared belief is based on the knowledge possessed by the sages that the virtuous actions of any one benefit them all, it is – I conjecture – not merely harmony but concord. I guess that a *full* definition of concord would have read: 'shared belief about the affairs of life, brought about by knowledge of common goods'. The short formula 'knowledge of common goods' simply picks out that element in the full definition which *distinguishes* concord from harmony, neglecting to specify e.g. the requirement that concord be shared between persons (it is not credible that such a requirement was not accepted by the Stoics).[42]

The details of this account of friendship and concord cannot be presumed to be Zeno's work. But Stob. II 93.19–94.6 is Arius Didymus' core statement about the community with one another enjoyed by the wise and morally good, and as such likely to have Zenonian ancestry. And unless Zeno himself had coupled friendship and concord in such a way as to suggest that friendship was to be understood in terms of concord, it is hard to conceive that such an account would have been elaborated. If the account is a fair reflection of what Zeno had in mind, it will follow that for him love brings about concord just inasmuch as it brings about friendship: what causes the coming about of state of affairs *S* thereby causes the coming about of the *definiens* of *S*.

VII

The connection between love and freedom is more problematical. Stoicism took freedom to be a moral characteristic: 'the power of

[42] I have put the argument for thinking that the account of concord (ὁμόνοια) as 'knowledge of goods' is not the complete definition to which the Stoics would have subscribed, but simply the most distinctive element in the complete definition. But there is an argument on the other side. This derives from reflection on the probability that the Stoic thinking about friendship and concord recorded by Arius Didymus exploits Platonic resources very heavily – indeed, it is almost a commentary on Plato (who must here be taken to include also the author of questionably Platonic dialogues such as *Alcibiades* I and *Cleitophon*). See Further Appendix E.

independent action' (D.L. VII 121). Very likely it is this moral freedom which Zeno in the *Republic* denied to all except the morally good (D.L. VII 33), and very likely for the Socratic reason that none but the good and wise choose to do what they really want.[43] It is hard to see how this has anything to do with love or friendship.

More sense can be made of what Athenaeus reports if we take freedom as political freedom, construed as the freedom of the *state* from tyrannical rule or from subjection to a foreign power. This is how Athenaeus himself understood Zeno, as becomes clear when we continue the quotation (561 C–562 A):

> Pontianus said that Zeno of Citium took Love to be a god who brings about friendship and freedom, and again concord, but nothing else. That is why in the *Republic* he said that Love is a god, there as a helper in furthering the safety of the city. But that those who preceded Zeno in philosophy also knew Love as a holy being, separated from everything ignoble, is clear from the fact that in the gymnasia statues are erected of him along with Hermes and Heracles, the first presiding over *logos*, the second over strength: when these are united, friendship and concord are born; and for those who pursue them it is by means of them that the noblest freedom also grows. The Athenians were so far from supposing that Love presides over any sexual intercourse, that although the Academy is quite obviously consecrated to Athena, they have put up a statue of Love right there and make sacrifices to him along with her. The people of Thespiae celebrate the Festival of Love ('Ερωτίδια) as they [sc. the Athenians] do the Athenaea or Elians the Olympia or Rhodians the Festival of the Sun ('Αλίεια). And in general, Love is honoured at offerings made at the public

[43] Although the evidence that this was the Stoic rationale of the doctrine is not as strong as could be desired, the coincidence of thought in Dio *Or.* XIV 16 [= *SVF* III 356] and Philo *quod omnis probus liber* II p. 454.12 ff. Mang. [= *SVF* III 362; cf. p. 454.31 ff. = *SVF* III 363] does not leave the matter in much doubt, given the Stoic cast of the definition of freedom in Dio (knowledge of what is permitted and what is prevented), the syllogistic pattern of the pieces of reasoning presented by Philo, and their close dependence on the well-attested Stoic thesis that the morally good man does all things well (especially as developed by Arius Didymus *apud* Stob. II 99.9–100.2).

> expense. The Spartans make preliminary sacrifices to Love before the troops are drawn up in line of battle, because they believe that safety and victory depend on the friendship of those who are drawn up alongside each other. Again, the Cretans order their line of battle so that the most handsome of the citizens are alongside each other, and by means of them make sacrifice to Love, as Sosicrates records. The Thebans' so-called Sacred Band is composed of lovers and their boy-friends, indicating the awesomeness of the god, as they embrace a glorious death in preference to an ignoble and reprehensible life. The Samians, as Erxias says in his *History of Colophon*, on dedicating a gymnasium to Love, called the festival they introduced in his honour the Festival of Freedom (Ἐλευθέρια). It was through this god that the Athenians, too, got their freedom; and the Peisistratids, after they were thrown out, were the first to try to slander the acts which concern this god.

If we follow Athenaeus, our interpretation will look to the example of the Spartans and the Cretans, of Harmodius and Aristogeiton and of the Sacred Band. Love inspires the mutual commitment between citizens which is required if a despot is to be overthrown, or if morale is to remain strong in time of crisis and the state to be saved from external threat. On this view, Zeno's inclusion of freedom among the benefits secured by love is motivated by republicanism. He shares the traditional Greek commitment to freedom from tyranny, whether internal or external. And he cares for freedom as a property of the city itself, not just as a characteristic of individuals.

Athenaeus' view of what Zeno was saying is consonant both with the Spartan ethos of the *Republic* (cf. Section IV above) and with its Platonic model: the Spartan state and the community of the guardians are institutions designed for war. But there is a difficulty in supposing that Zeno' s state was similarly militaristic. The sources breathe no hint of militarism. And one of Philodemus' proofs of the authenticity of the *Republic* of Diogenes the Cynic consists in a report of a reference by Chrysippus in *his On Republic* to a statement of Diogenes 'on the uselessness of weapons' – which Chrysippus appears to have endorsed (*On the Stoics* col. XV 31–XVI 4). Scholars have plausibly inferred that Chrysippus' adoption of the idea probably reflects an assertion to the same effect in Zeno's *Republic*.[44] If so, the connection between love and freedom suggested by Athenaeus' comparative material will not be Zenonian, for it is mediated by the willingness of lovers to fight for their country.

Why should Diogenes the Cynic have condemned weapons as useless? The doxographical account of his teaching at D.L. VI 70–1 may provide some material pertinent to an answer. The central theme of Cynic teaching was ἄσκησις (exercise or training), or πόνος (suffering or struggle): the only training or struggle worth anything was directed towards virtue and moral freedom. From D.L. VI 71 it sounds as though Diogenes may have used a military metaphor in this connection, for training is described as 'capable of outright victory over anything'. The text continues: 'Therefore instead of useless struggles we should choose those in accordance with nature – and live happily.' There seems a fair chance that these ideas provide the context of the remark about weapons. Military campaigns and the use of weapons they require are no doubt among the forms of struggle Diogenes counts as useless. Only *moral* struggle gives us worthwhile victories.[45] The needlessness of weapons is likewise something stressed by Crates in his poem (D.L. VI 85) on the ideal city – as pointless for the self-sufficient Cynic. His 'citizens' have in their knapsacks thyme, garlic, figs and loaves:

> Consequently they do not go to war with one another for these things, nor have they acquired weapons to fight for cash or for glory.

The point, I take it, is that what is necessary for self-sufficiency the wise man already has – so there is no point in fighting over it; what

[44] So Baldry, *JHS* 79 (1959), p. 10 with n. 12.

[45] On this theme in Diogenes see M.-O. Goulet-Cazé, *L'Ascèse Cynique* (Paris 1986); cf. also G. Giannantoni, *Socraticorum Reliquiae* (Rome 1985), Vol. III, Nota 50, with pertinent texts in Vol. II, V B 290–331. Particularly relevant is V B 299 (Maxim. Tyr. *Philosoph.* XXXVI 5–6), which treats going on military expeditions as one of many futile enterprises eschewed by Diogenes, but undertaken typically out of greed (πλεονεξία), and which records the following anecdote: 'When Greece was at war, and everyone attacking everyone else, 'of those who formerly brought War plentiful in tears upon each other', he alone brought in a truce, unarmed among the armed.' This is, of course, Diogenizing rather than Diogenes.

is not necessary (cash, glory) is not necessary – so there is no point in fighting for that either.[46]

Zeno was evidently in a measure of agreement with the Cynic view of the exclusive importance of moral virtue for an individual. This is presumably why he followed the Cynics in rejecting in the *Republic* 'the ordinary education' (D.L. VII 32; cf. VI 73, 103–4), as did the Spartans according to Xenophon (*Lac. Pol.* 2.1) – and indeed on any view of the ἀγωγή. Insistence by him on the importance for a person's happiness of virtue and virtue alone may therefore be what is ultimately reflected in Chrysippus' repetition of Diogenes' remark about the uselessness of weapons.

So far as we can tell, the Cynics in rejecting war did not consider whether political freedom might not supply a valid reason for fighting as money and glory do not. The values in terms of which they conduct their argument are solely individual, not communal. From Zeno's endorsement of the Cynic position we could not infer that he had likewise left the issue of political freedom out of account, particularly in view of the fact that in giving a key role to *concord* the *Republic* indubitably appeals to a value that is not purely individual. Nonetheless the Cynic antinomianism of so much of the *Republic* places the burden of proof on those who want to maintain, with respect to any particular communal value, that Zeno gave it weight in his scheme of things. The balance of probability is that he viewed the idea of fighting for one's country with Cynic aversion for exactly the Cynic's reasons – and that this is a point at which he makes a radical departure from the outlook both of Plato's *Republic* and of Spartan, and in general Greek, civic ideology.[47]

[46] Cf. Cleanthes' *Hymn to Zeus* 27–8 (Stob. I 26, 16–17), which makes glory and gain the first two of the foolish pursuits ordinary men engage in.

[47] Early Stoicism of course at some point developed an account of how the wise man should conduct himself in existing circumstances, where the conditions necessary for the emergence of the ideal community were not satisfied (see Appendix D). In this context the Stoics were prepared both to make service to one's country a valid motive for action (e.g. political activity: Stob. II 111.5–9; marriage: *ibid.* II 94.14–17, suicide: D.L. VII 130) and to make the wise man the only true general (Stob. II 102.11–13). This last doctrine perhaps goes back to Zeno himself. Plutarch (*Aratus* 23) has a nice anecdote about Persaeus: dislodged by the young Aratus from the Acrocorinth where he had been installed by Antigonus as garrison commander, he is alleged to have said of the idea that the wise man is the only true general that it used to be his

Is there available an explanation of how Zeno thinks love brings about freedom which does not require the focus on war inherent in Athenaeus' account? An alternative approach might be to suppose that the only thing love produces strictly speaking is friendship; and that what Zeno then claimed was that by virtue of the friendship of its citizens his state achieved ideals of concord and freedom to which political theorists and publicists in fourth- and third-century Greece very generally subscribed. We might conjecture that concord and freedom had become almost conventional goals of many high-minded political programmes, so that (1) a philosopher could understandably regard himself as obliged to show that they could be secured by introduction of the political system he was recommending, and yet (2) they need not be ideals which represented anything distinctive or fundamental in his own scheme of things. On this view, friendship will have been what really mattered to Zeno, not concord and freedom. So even if there is a military dimension to the pursuit of concord and freedom, it need not be regarded as the significant element in Zeno's thought which it has to be on Athenaeus' account.

The coupling of concord and freedom in political rhetoric is easily documented. I select just two from many possible examples. Isocrates in the fourth century makes frequent reference to his own manifesto calling for concord among the Greeks and campaigns against the barbarians (e.g. *Panath.* 13, *Antidosis* 77, *Philip* 16, *Paneg.* 85, 104), or, as he phrases the ideas at *Paneg.* 106, describing the democracies installed by Athens in the member states of the Delian league, they continued 'free as regards the barbarians, without civil strife (στάσις) as regards themselves'. In third-century Athens the same rhetoric is employed by the anti-Macedonian party led by Chremonides. His decree of 268/7 – still in Zeno's lifetime – establishing a treaty between Athens and Sparta speaks *inter alia* of the creation of a 'common concord' among the Greeks that revives the old friendship and alliance at the time of the Persian Wars, in which they 'acquired reputation for themselves and achieved freedom for the other Greeks'. And the decree for Chremonides' brother Glaucon, about the same

favourite among Zeno's doctrines – but the young man from Sicyon had now taught him a lesson which had changed his mind.

time or a little later, establishes a cult of Zeus Eleutherios (god of freedom) and of Concord at Plataea, site of the great victory over the Persians in 480 B.C., again recalling the struggle 'against the barbarians in defence of the freedom of the Greeks'.[48]

One has only to reproduce this rhetoric to see the inadequacy of the alternative account of why Zeno might have talked in the *Republic* of concord and freedom. The rhetoric, although conventional, is irredeemably bellicose. If Zeno in any sense meant it, it would be hard to avoid concluding that the *Republic* *was* militaristic, contrary to the rest of the evidence. If he did not, then the stature of the book is diminished; and we are required to believe that, while happy to tear down political conventions on an ambitious scale elsewhere in the *Republic*, at just this point he paid lip-service to them. Exchanging idolization of Sparta and the Sacred Band for pan-Hellenist ideology has not enabled us to arrive at a more acceptable interpretation.

We have therefore reached an impasse. While there is no difficulty in accepting that Zeno's *Republic* made friendship and concord something love could bring about, its relation to freedom is deeply problematical.

There is a straightforward solution to the puzzle: Athenaeus' report is wrong – Zeno never did claim that love had any connection with freedom.

This solution is not arbitrary. *If* Zeno had said what Athenaeus attributes to him, he must have been talking of political freedom. Yet later Stoics never attempt to elaborate a concept of political freedom, even though they devote strenuous energy to defining and developing all the other concepts we know Zeno deployed in

[48] For presentation and discussion of the evidence on this topic see R. Étienne and M. Piérart, 'Un décret du koinon des Hellénes á Platées en l'honneur de Glaucon, fils d' 'Eteocles, d'Athènes', *Bull. Corresp. Hell.* 99 (1975) 51–75 (which ranges much more widely than might be inferred from its title); W.C. West, 'Hellenic Homonoia and the New Decree from Plataea', *GRBS* 18 (1977) 307–19. The decree of Chremonides can be found in H. Schmitt, *Die Staatsverträge des Altertums* III (Munich 1969), no. 476, pp. 129–33. Erskine (*The Hellenistic Stoa*, Ch.4) tries to make a close connection between what Athenaeus tells us of Zeno's commitment to concord and freedom and Chremonides' anti-Macedonian rhetoric. In my view the attempt fails: the evidence connecting Zeno with Athenian and Macedonian politics is flimsy anecdotal stuff, and as the articles cited above show, Chremonides was exploiting a long tradition of pan-Hellenic rhetoric, not utopian philosophy.

the *Republic*, including friendship and concord. The obvious reason for their not doing so is that Zeno said nothing there about political freedom.

If we look again at Athenaeus' text we can see just how he could have come to insert a reference to freedom into Zeno's teaching (561C):

> Pontianus said that Zeno of Citium took love to be a god who brings about friendship and freedom, and again concord, but nothing else. That is why in the *Republic* he said that Love is a god, there as a helper in furthering the safety of the city.

I suggest that Athenaeus has himself extrapolated from the genuinely Zenonian thesis about the safety of the city to a claim about freedom: i.e. Zeno really did say that love furthers the safety of the city, whereas it is Athenaeus who has turned this into a proposition about freedom. The transformation is a very natural one to make – so natural that he was doubtless not conscious that it *was* a transformation.

The safety of a city or an alliance can be conceived of in two ways: either as its security against external assaults on its independence; or as its security from στάσις and internal disintegration. Greek authors often have the first conception in mind when they talk of safety. So e.g. Thucydides (II 60.4), Plato (*Prot.* 354 B), and Isocrates when he says of the Athenians and Spartans at the time of the Persian Wars that they 'did not court the favour of the barbarians for the enslavement of the Greeks, but were of concordant mind (ὁμονοοῦντες) about the common safety' (*Paneg.* 85). But the second conception is also much in evidence, as e.g. in Andocides (*Myst.* 140), Plato (*Rep.* 433 B) and notably Aristotle, who, in devoting Book V of the *Politics* to study of 'destructions' and 'preservations' (σωτηρίαι) of constitutions (V 1, 1301a19–25), is mostly concerned with threats to internal stability. On the first conception, preoccupation with safety comes to the same thing as preoccupation with freedom, as Isocrates' words suggest. Not so on the second conception. It is, of course, plausible to argue or assume that a state or alliance not secure from στάσις will be less able and willing to fight for independence or resist assaults against its freedom from external domination. But that is a separate point. And it is perfectly possible for a politician or a theorist to focus attention on concord and security from στάσις without showing much if any interest in freedom from external domination. Plato in *Republic* IV and Aristotle in *Politics* V are cases in point. Their example perhaps makes it more likely, and certainly shows it possible, that Zeno also connected concord solely with safety in the sense of internal stability. Athenaeus' mistake will have been to suppose that he was thinking of the first conception of safety, and so of its inevitable concomitant, freedom from military threats without.

VIII

Zeno's *Republic*, I have argued, is a work which continued the tradition and style of political philosophy familiar from Plato's *Republic*. Zeno envisages a community in the ordinary sense of the word, but a community that is as perfect as may be, by virtue of its communist institutions and the moral character of its citizens, and the friendship and concord which exists among them. His work is much shorter than Plato's – one book against ten – primarily because he covers only a few of the topics of Plato's *Republic*, but also because he aims at a greater simplicity: no elaborate education system, no division into classes. Simplicity is Zeno's recipe for goodness and concord.[49]

Brevity and simplicity are Laconic as well as Cynic virtues. And I have suggested that Zeno's *Republic* constitutes a kind of Spartan reply to Plato's Athenian Stranger, or (as I suspect Sphaerus presented it) Lycurgus' answer to the Socrates of Plato's *Republic*. Zeno, like the Spartans, makes love a distinctive element in his political system. But it is a radically sublimated form of love (as in Plato); it is homosexual, but probably it can equally be heterosexual; and it has no connection with war.

[49] On brevity as a hallmark of Zeno's style of thought see my article 'The syllogisms of Zeno of Citium', *Phronesis* 28 (1983) 31–58.

3

The cosmic city

I

On the banks of the Bug in the Crimaea, a little above its confluence with the Dnieper (Borysthenes as the Greeks called it), stood the ancient Milesian colony of Olbia or Borysthenes. Among other distinctions it practised the worship of Achilles;[1] it supplies us with a precious piece of early evidence about the Dionysiac dimension of Orphism;[2] and it provides the setting for Dio Chrysostom's 36th *logos*.[3]

Dio tells us at the outset (§1) that he was visiting the city in the course of a journey through Scythia to the Getae, whose ethnography was the subject of a work by him now lost. The expedition took him from the Greek world to barbarians beyond its limits. And the *logos* soon makes it clear that Borysthenes represents a

[1] Cf. E. Belin de Ballu, *Olbia: cité antique du littoral nord de la mer noire* (Leiden 1972) 77–82, 139–40, 164–5; further information in C.P. Jones, *The Roman World of Dio Chrysostom* (Cambridge MA/London 1978) 62–3, 178–9.

[2] Cf. M.L. West, 'The Orphics of Olbia', *ZPE* 45 (1982) 17–29; a brief summary of the evidence in G.S. Kirk, J.E. Raven, M. Schofield, *The Presocratic Philosophers* (Cambridge 1983, second edition) 30, 208 n. 1.

[3] I.e. 36th according to the tradition followed in von Arnim's edition and reproduced in the Loeb. On the *Borysthenitikos logos* I have consulted H. von Arnim, *Leben und Werke des Dio von Prusa* (Berlin 1898), esp. 482–9 (excellent value); P. Desideri, *Dione di Prusa* (Messina/Firenze 1978), esp. 318–27, 361–71 (useful notes); and C.P. Jones, *The Roman World of Dio Chrysostom*, ch. 7 (historically informative, but fundamentally and without argument misidentifies Dio's purpose as that of 'making the Olbians a community of ideal virtue and self-sufficiency' (p. 63), when his point is that they are poised between Hellenism and barbarism). The interpretation developed in Section I was mostly worked out before I read M.B. Trapp, 'Plato's *Phaedrus* in Second-Century Greek Literature', in D.A. Russell (ed.), *Antonine Literature* (Oxford 1990), and I am much encouraged by the convergence between our readings. I have profited from his comments on the first draft of Section I, and have gratefully borrowed his observations on §§18–19 (see p. 151 of his article) and on a number of other points.

point of contact between Greeks and barbarians in more than a physical and commercial sense. By virtue of its history and situation and of the constitution of its population it is a sort of hybrid of the Greek and the barbarian.

Thus the city 'is always in a state of war' (§4); and to emphasize the point Dio makes it the victim of a Scythian raid the very day before the discussions with the Borystheneans he purports to be recording (§15). It 'has often been captured, most recently and on the largest scale no more than 150 years ago' – by the Getae, so it transpires (§4). According to Dio the result of this last occupation was that Borysthenes ceased to function as a city, and such of the Greek population as survived were dispersed. It is implied that the site was taken over by 'barbarians'; and contact with Greece came to an end, since the Scythians could not speak Greek and 'had neither the ambition nor the knowledge to establish a trading-centre after the Greek manner'. Eventually the Greek colonists collected and made it a city again. Dio suggests this was because the Scythians wanted trade to resume (§5). But the city was now confined to a portion of the old site; its houses were poor, the new part of the wall mean and weak, and funerary monuments and temple statues all mutilated (§6). Dio does not offer a connected account along similar lines of the cultural consequences of the Borystheneans' historical and topographical situation. But he drops hints. They dress like Scythians, even if their long hair and beards are reminiscent of Homer's Greeks (§§7, 17). They no longer speak Greek clearly, because they live in the midst of barbarians (§9). While they revere Homer and a few know Plato, they are largely ignorant of other poetry and philosophy, although they are truly Greek in their desire to know more (§§9, 14, 16, 26). The elderly Hieroson is represented as defensively but elegantly self-conscious about their 'barbarism' (§§24–6). It is accordingly a nice touch when Dio concludes his *logos* by clothing Stoic cosmological theory in a myth he attributes to Zoroaster and the Magi (§§39–61) and describes as a 'barbarian song' – apologizing for not offering something 'Greek and graceful' (§43).

Both the subject and the method of the *logos* are matched by Dio to the Borysthenes he has portrayed. His subject is the city. The precarious hold Borysthenes has on the status of city and on

Hellenism makes a visit to it an appropriate occasion to raise the philosophical question: what is a city? Dio introduces the topic in two stages. He starts where the Borystheneans are: with poetry, with Homer and with war. And he puts to his first interlocutor the shocking question: 'Do you think Homer is a better poet than Phocylides?' (§10) The interlocutor has never heard of Phocylides. Dio therefore proceeds to contrast Phocylides' manner and matter with Homer's way of 'stringing together a long continuous poem' and 'going through a single battle continuously in more than 5000 verses' (§§10–12). He focuses on one of Phocylides' maxims of 'two or three verses' in particular (§13):

> This too is a saying of Phocylides: a city on a rock,
> living in order, although small is better than mad Nineveh.

> In comparison with the entire *Iliad* and *Odyssey* are not these verses noble to those who pay attention to what they hear? Or was it more to your advantage to hear about the leapings and rushings of Achilles, and about his voice, how by his utterance alone he would rout the Trojans? Is it more beneficial for you to learn that by heart than this truth, that a small city set on a rugged rock is better and more fortunate, provided it lives in order, than a great city in a smooth and level plain, if its inhabitants are foolish men who live in disorder and lawlessly?

Phocylides is a poet. But the economy and discipline of his style, and its appropriateness to the austerity of his doctrine, already anticipate the Stoicism now to be introduced. For having put the city on the agenda for discussion, Dio moves to the second phase of his dialectic: a direct philosophical discussion of what a city is and what a good city is, largely Stoic in substance although with significant references to Platonic doctrine (§§18–23). An interruption by Hieroson succeeds in turning the *logos* subsequently in a different direction: but more of that anon.

The method Dio adopts in this *logos* is Platonic in inspiration. This is doubly appropriate to the Borystheneans. (1) Wedded as they are to Homer and to war (§§9–10), they need the shock of a challenge to their allegiances such as Plato's Socrates administers to his interlocutors, and they may respond to the mixture of argument and myth characteristic of Platonic dialogues of the middle period (cf. §27). (2) Insofar as they have any antecedent sense of what philosophy is, it comes from Plato (§§26–7).

The reader is left in no doubt that Dio's method is Platonic. He begins (§18) by stressing the importance of asking the τί ἐστι; question ('What is ... ?') about a thing if one wants to grasp what sort of thing it is (ὁποῖόν τι ἐστιν). In similarly Socratic manner he gives an example of what he has in mind (§19): in the case of *man* (ἄνθρωπος) we need to know not just how to use the word but how to produce the right answer to the τί ἐστι; question: 'mortal rational animal'. His procedure is by this stage in the *logos* scarcely surprising, given that the whole story of his encounter with the Borystheneans is presented in the style of a Platonic dialogue. Dio evidently has a particular model in mind: the *Phaedrus*. Like Socrates and Phaedrus at the beginning of the *Phaedrus*, at the start of *Or*. XXXVI (§1) Dio is strolling outside the city – in fact by the Hypanis or Bug, as Socrates and Phaedrus walked down by the Ilissus. Both prefaces dwell on matters of topography with some insistence (§§1–7). Socrates' rare excursion from the city is evidently highly symbolic. No less symbolically Dio and the Borystheneans *enter* the city to pursue their discussion about the city, for what I have called the second and overtly philosophical phase of Dio's dialectic (§§16–17). *Or*. XXXVI culminates in an elaborate myth of Zeus's chariot and team of horses which recalls the myth of the horses and charioteer that concludes the first part of the *Phaedrus* (§§39ff.). In his portrayal of Callistratus, the first interlocutor, Dio reinforces at an early stage in his *logos* the reader's sense of an echo of Plato in general and the *Phaedrus* in particular. Callistratus is described in the glowing terms apt for an ideal Platonic ἐρώμενος (§8). But at the same time Dio suggests that homosexual love in Borysthenes is in danger of perversion, since the barbarians are likely to take it up (*ibid*.). One is passingly and unemphatically reminded of the *Phaedrus*' attempt to discriminate good from bad ἔρως. Finally, the very insistence on the need to begin by getting clear what one is talking about (§18) parallels the opening of Socrates' first speech in the *Phaedrus* (237 B–C).

What is required of Dio in these circumstances is not a set of his own nostrums about the idea of the city, but an authoritative statement of the teaching of Greece and of philosophy on the subject. In the first instance this turns out to be not Platonic but Stoic doctrine: Hieroson, who knows his Plato, declares himself and the Borystheneans inexperienced in 'this more precise philosophy', which is the way Stoicism was often perceived in antiquity (§26); and we have sufficient parallels in other sources to be sure of the Stoic provenance of the major theses Dio ascribes to 'our people' (τῶν ἡμετέρων, §29) or to 'the theory of the philosophers' (§38).

Thus he begins by telling the Borystheneans that 'they' [reference unspecific] say that the city is 'a group of men (ἄνθρωποι) living in the same place who are administered by law' (§20). This is a version of the Stoic definition recorded by Clement (*Strom.* IV 26):[4]

> The Stoics say that the universe (οὐρανός) is in the proper sense a city, but that those here on earth are not – they are called cities, but are not really. For a city or a people is something morally good, an organization or group of men administered by law which exhibits refinement (ἀστεῖον).[5]

Dio draws a characteristically Stoic consequence from the definition, couched mostly in Stoic vocabulary (§20):

> It is immediately evident, therefore, that this expression [sc. 'city'] is not appropriate for any of the so-called cities which are foolish and lawless. So the poet would have spoken not even of Nineveh as a city, since it is mad. For just as he who does not have rationality as an attribute is not a human being, so what does not have being law-abiding as a property is not a city. And if it were senseless and disorderly, it could never be law-abiding.

This in fact begins to spell out the connection between the definition of city and the thesis that cities on earth are not true cities which Clement assumes but does not articulate.

Actually Dio never goes so far as to assert unequivocally what we may call Clement's thesis: that cities on earth are not really

[4] The relation between the standard Stoic definition and Cleanthes' syllogism on the city is discussed in Appendix F.

[5] On the meaning of ἀστεῖον in this and other early Stoic texts see Appendix G.

cities; nor its complement: that the universe itself is the only true city. There seem to be two reasons for this, one largely internal to Dio's particular purposes in *Or.* XXXVI and one reflecting a famous project in Greek political philosophy.

Dio represents himself in this part of the *logos* as having a political purpose – to encourage a positive vision of how an earthly city might at least achieve a degree of equitability, even if it will inevitably fall short of being a community governed by divine law (§23):

> Of the rest [sc. communities other than the society of gods with each other] all everywhere are almost without qualification in error and morally bad in comparison with the supreme righteousness of the divine and blessed law and correct administration. Nonetheless for present purposes let us take a supply of examples of the community which is equitable relative to one which is totally corrupt, just as among persons who are all ill, we compare the one who has a very light case with the one who is in a very bad condition.

I take it that he has earlier given a hint of what such a community might be like (§21):

> Someone might perhaps enquire whether, when the rulers and leaders are wise and persons of judgment, and the rest of the population are administered in accordance with their decisions in a sane and law-abiding way, such a community should be called sane and law-abiding and really a city – because of those who administer it: just as we might perhaps call a chorus musical, provided that its leader was musical, and provided that the others followed him and uttered no sound contrary to the melody or only slight and indistinct ones. For no one knows of a good city, made up entirely of good elements – neither a mortal one that came to be in the past, nor is one that is to be one day in the future worth conceiving of – unless it be a city of the blessed gods in heaven.

Dio toys with the idea that one might have an earthly community which counts as law-abiding and so satisfies the Stoic definition of a city, without yet being a *good* city, i.e. a city made up entirely of good persons. The idea is not his own, of course, but Plato's. It is Plato's *Republic* which envisages a good city where only the rulers are wise. In effect, therefore, Dio is inviting the Borystheneans to join him in doing some political philosophy in the Platonic style.[6]

The invitation is politely declined. Hieroson and the Borystheneans are much more excited by what Dio has said about 'the divine administration' of the universe (§§25–26; cf. 22). Dio is told (§27):

> If you are willing to do all of us a favour, postpone your *logos* on the mortal city . . . and speak instead about the divine city or administration, whichever you prefer to call it – tell us what it is like, aiming as closely as possible at the nobility of Plato in your diction, as you seemed to us to be doing just now.

This sets the agenda for the rest of the *logos* (and indeed of our chapter); the topic prescribed of course lends itself much better than political theory (the '*logos* on the mortal city') to the elevated style preferred by the Borystheneans. It is presumably not just Dio's diction when speaking of the divine city which is supposed to have captured the Borystheneans' imagination. For at the heart of the conception of the mutual society of the gods that Dio has sketched is the idea of a form of common life in which there is no internal strife nor the possibility of defeat by external forces, but 'a dance of happiness danced with understanding and supreme wisdom' (§22) – and yet in which men may have the sort of share that children have in the adult world. This idea is diametrically opposed to the Borystheneans' current situation in every dimension Dio has got us to think of. No wonder they are so attracted to it. As often, the dispossessed prefer the prospect of heaven to political thought.

II

Prima facie it would seem odd to begin an investigation into the early Stoic doctrine of the cosmic city with discussion of an

[6] I am indebted to Michael Trapp for pointing out to me the Platonic provenance and intentions of this stretch of text.

epideixis by a sophist written at the turn of the first and second centuries A.D.[7] Certainly Dio is not regarded as a prime source for much else in Stoicism.[8] Section I has argued that his particular purposes in the *logos Borysthenitikos* make him an unexpectedly reliable witness to orthodox Stoic views on the city and the cosmos. Von Arnim was therefore justified in excerpting substantial portions of the speech to illustrate Stoic thought on these topics in *SVF*. On the other hand Dio's literary sophistication and ambition are such that, once we move beyond the definition of the city which he reports, inferences from what he says to what the early Stoics held are never straightforward.

Fortunately we have just sufficient doxographic evidence (discussed in Sections III and IV) to be able to identify the shape and philosophical context of the original Stoic theory of the cosmic city. We then consider the evidence in Philodemus for Chrysippus' introduction of the doctrine in Book III of *On nature*, and attempt a reconstruction of the main sequence of ideas in *On nature* from the numerous fragments and references to it in Plutarch (Section V). We will then be in a position to examine Dio's account of the theory in §§29–38 of his *logos* (Section VI).

III

When Diogenes the Cynic described himself as κοσμοπολίτης, 'citizen of the universe', he implied that he was at home nowhere – except in the universe itself. There can be little doubt that the Stoic doctrine of the cosmic city was developed as an explication of this dictum.[9] The element of comfort it contains is like-

[7] Some (including Dio himself) would object to the designation 'sophist': see e.g. Jones, *The Roman World of Dio Chrysostom*. For a nuanced and convincing discussion of Dio's individual mix of sophistry and philosophy see J.L. Moles, 'The career and conversion of Dio Chrysostom', *JHS* 98 (1978) 79–100, which leaves me of the opinion that 'sophist' is the best single term to describe a figure so preoccupied with self-presentation and with its literary and philosophical resonances as Dio emerges from his analysis.

[8] Cf. P.A. Brunt, 'From Epictetus to Arrian', *Athenaeum* 55 (1977) 19–48, at p. 39: it is ' certain that Dio Chrysostom was too much of a sophist and an eclectic to be regarded, except where confirmation can be found, as an expositor of Stoic ethics'.

[9] For discussion of Diogenes' cosmopolitanism and its Stoic interpretation see Appendix H.

wise mirrored in the systematic context in Stoicism to which the doctrine belongs. It is part of the Stoics' teaching on divine providence.

The clearest evidence of this comes from Cicero's *de natura deorum*. Book II, devoted to Stoic theology, is explicitly organized on a four section plan. The Stoics 'teach first that there are gods, next what they are like, then that the universe is administered by them, and finally that they pay attention to the affairs of men' (*ND* II 3). Cicero eventually reaches the fourth topic at §154:[10]

> It remains for me to teach by way of conclusion that all the things there are in the universe that are used by men have been created and provided for the sake of men.

The first argument he offers for the thesis is based on the doctrine of the cosmic city (*ibid.*):

> In the first place the universe itself was created for the sake of gods and men, and the things it contains were provided and contrived for the enjoyment of men. For the universe is as it were the common home of gods and men, or a city that belongs to both. For they alone live according to justice and law by the use of reason. So just as it must be supposed that Athens and Sparta were founded for the sake of the Athenians and the Spartans, and all the things contained in those cities are rightly said to belong to those peoples, so whatever things are contained in the entire universe must be supposed to belong to gods and men.

The passage has a clear inferential structure. The fundamental premiss is the proposition (1) that it is true of men and gods alone that by use of reason they live in accordance with justice and law. This proposition is taken to license the inference that (2) men and gods form a community or a city. It is then assumed (3) that the

[10] There is general if not unanimous agreement by commentators that this *is* the formal starting-point for discussion of the fourth topic of the book, but equally Cicero is often accused of muddying the waters by actually beginning to talk about it at §133. See e.g. J.B. Mayor, *M. Tulli Ciceronis De Natura Deorum* (Cambridge 1883) II 253 (ad §133); A.S. Pease, *M. Tulli Ciceronis De Natura Deorum* (Cambridge MA 1958) II 894 (ad §132), 949 (ad §154); A.J. Kleywegt, *Ciceros Arbeitsweise im zweiten und dritten Buch der Schrift De Natura Deorum* (Groningen 1961) 92–116.

location of this city is the universe itself. Argument is supplied for the further premiss (4) that cities are created for their inhabitants. From this general proposition (4), together with (2) and (3), it is taken to follow (5) that the universe (with its contents) was created for the sake of men and gods, the city for the sake of its citizens. The extent of the anthropocentrism of the teleology in (5) varies in Cicero's different formulations. Probably we should take the most careful of them to be the most authoritative, viz. the initial statement that 'all the things in this universe that are used by men have been created and provided for the sake of men'.[11]

The argument Cicero records looks like a reliable piece of doxography. In *ND* II his brief is to expound Stoic doctrine; and although he allows himself plenty of scope for elaboration of the Stoic material of the book in his own individual style, the present passage is not a case in point. Its faithful doxographic status is confirmed by an extract from Arius Didymus in Eusebius (*Praep. ev.* XV 15):

> The universe is said to be an organization of heaven and air and earth and sea and the natures within them. The universe is called also the habitation of gods and men and the organization of gods and men and the things which have come into being for their sake. For just as city is spoken of in two ways, as the habitation and as the organization of the inhabitants along with the citizens, so also the universe is as it were a city consisting of gods and men, the gods exercising the leadership, the men subordinate. Community exists between them because they partake in reason, which is natural law; and all else has come into being for their sake. In consequence of which it must be believed that

[11] The careful formulation makes it easy for the Stoics to avoid the charge (cf. M. Dragona-Monachou, *The Stoic Arguments for the Existence and Providence of the Gods* (Athens 1976) 156–9) that the anthropocentrism here is incompatible with their thesis that man is created in order to contemplate the universe (*ND* II 37) and their argument that it would be insane to think it was men's, not the gods', abode (*ND* II 17). The idea of the cosmic city is introduced in the context of arguments for providence at two other points in *ND* II. The train of thought in the first (II 78–9) is hard to understand (cf. Mayor *ad loc.*), or at any rate to accept as genuine Stoic reasoning as presented. Perhaps some garbling has occurred. The line of reasoning in the second context (II 133) appears to be no more than a simplified and more rhetorical version of the argument at II 154, and actually omits explicit reference to a city.

> the god who administers the wholes exercises providence for men, being beneficent, kind, well-disposed to men, just and having all the virtues.

Arius Didymus presents the same material as Cicero mostly in the same order, although the argumentative structure is less explicit. He is more intent on spelling out a *definition* of *the universe* in the light of the doctrine of the cosmic city than in drawing out the teleological conclusion which is the focus of the Cicero text. But it is made clear that (2) follows from (1). Assumption (3) is given the lion' s share of attention, no doubt because of Arius Didymus' definitional preoccupations. (5) is not formally derived from (2)–(4), and indeed (4) is not spelled out at all. Nonetheless (5) is indicated – albeit sketchily – in the text, for an unspecific version of it is tacked on rather lamely after Arius Didymus has dealt with (3) and the inference from (1) to (2): 'and all else has come into being for their sake'. And it is followed by a more general statement of what is described as the consequence that god exercises providential care for men. We may reasonably infer that lying behind this text was originally a line of argument as explicitly concerned with the deduction of (5) from (1) to (4) as the one we find in Cicero, subsequently obscured by the displacement of (5) as the main focus of the text by the definitions Arius Didymus begins with. Elsewhere he associates the definitions with Chrysippus (Stob. I 184.8–11); even if Arius is himself responsible for formulating them as such, the attribution gives grounds for thinking that the material (including the argument from (1) to (5)) on which the formulations are based derives from Chrysippus.

IV

Why should rational beings who live in accordance with law and justice on that account constitute a community? Why is (2) taken to follow from (1)? The line of argument is set out step by step in another Ciceronian text (*Leg.* I 23):

> Since nothing is better than reason, and this exists in both man and god, man's first association with god is in reason. But those who have reason in common also have right reason in common. Since that is law, we men must also be

> reckoned to be associated with the gods in law. But further, those who have law in common have justice in common. But those who have these things in common must be held to belong to the same state (*civitas*).[12]

Cicero does not tell us that this is Stoic material he is producing; nor is *Leg.* I an exposition of Stoic doctrine in the way that *ND* II is conceived expressly as an account of Stoic theology, although it is clearly a reworking of basically Stoic material. The Stoic credentials of the present passage are supported by a similar passage in Marcus Aurelius (*Med.* IV 4)[13] as well as by the characteristic form of the argument. The conceptual connections Cicero indicates are of course attested in other texts of certain or probable Stoic provenance. In particular, the proposition that law is simply right reason employed in prescribing what should be done and

[12] Cicero speaks of 'state' (*civitas*), not 'commonwealth' (*res publica*); and in the immediate sequel adds an argument (whose Stoic credentials are not so secure) from obedience to a single ruler to the thesis that gods and men belong to a single state (*ibid.*). But he is presumably translating πόλις, and it would accordingly be rash to presume that the Stoic original of the argument from sharing reason involved a conception of the state rather than (as I shall argue) a community or commonwealth.

[13] Marcus argues (in a style more characteristic of Chrysippus than of himself): 'If mind is common to us, so also is reason, in virtue of which we are rational. If that is so, the reason which prescribes what is and is not to be done is also common. If that is so, law also is common; if that is so, we are citizens; if that is so, we partake in a kind of political system (πολιτεύματός τινος); if that is so, the universe is as it were a city. For what other common political system will anyone say the whole race of men partakes in? And if mind and our capacities for reason and law do not come from this common city, where do they come from?' What is remarkable in this passage is Marcus's revisionist treatment of the cosmic city as common not to gods and men, but to men alone – even though his version of the argument, like Cicero's, turns on the idea that those beings which have reason in common are fellow-citizens. So far as I can discover, this is a view of the cosmic city unique to Marcus: other Stoics of the Imperial era adhere to the conception traditional in the school which speaks of an organization of gods and men, e.g. Sen. *de otio* 4; Musonius Rufus *apud* Stob. III 74 9.2–14; Epict. *Diss.* I 9.4 (where θεοῦ is substituted for θεῶν) and many further references collected in Pease, *De Natura Deorum* II 950–1 (ad *ND* II 154). Here is striking evidence of Marcus' unorthodox disbelief in the doctrine of the kinship of man and god, remarked upon e.g. by R.B. Rutherford, *The Meditations of Marcus Aurelius: a Study* (Oxford 1989), ch. VI, esp. p. 227 (but Rutherford fails to note the omission of gods from the cosmic community in his discussion of IV 4, pp. 239–40, as also does G.R. Stanton, 'The cosmopolitan ideas of Epictetus and Marcus Aurelius', *Phronesis* 13 (1968) 183–95).

forbidding what should not be done is a securely Stoic and indeed Chrysippean thesis.[14]

If the Stoics had been content to construe the notion of law in a traditional way, whether conceived as positive law or otherwise, there would be no difficulty in seeing how the move from law to community or city would work. Law so conceived is the law *of* some community or city or state; and it derives its authority as law from the fact that it is somehow the voice of the city or community or state in question. But such a conception of the authority of law is precisely what the Stoics reject. For them that authority is not vested in the state, particularly not the state as we know it 'on earth'. The point of their equation of law with right reason is to identify an alternative source for its authority: not the state, but reason. Its effect is to internalize law, making it something like the voice of conscience or (as a still later moral tradition would put it) the moral law within. Yet in the argument for the cosmic city the Stoics appear to be wanting to have their cake and eat it. Having seemingly extruded all reference to the city or community or state from their account of law, they now try to reinstitute a connection.

Leg. I 23 evidently gives a key role in this context to the idea that reason, right reason, law and justice are possessed 'in common'. The idea requires scrutiny. For it does not in general follow that if two persons have some property in common, they thereby constitute a community. I have the name 'Schofield' and the designation 'author' in common with all other Schofields and authors. But it would be absurd to suggest that simply in virtue of this fact the Schofields and again authors form a community. Similarly if you and I share red cheeks and blue eyes, we do not on that account belong to any society. What entitles the Stoics to suppose that our both possessing reason causes us to do so?

The answer must turn on what philosophical conception of reason they accept. One widespread contemporary view makes reason a purely formal notion. To put the point in logical terms, on this view the proper scope of reason is restricted to inference and the assessment of the validity of inferences. The content of premisses and assessment of their truth lie outside its sphere of

[14] See Marcianus *Inst.* I 11.25, Plu. *Stoic. rep.* 1037 F, Stob. II 96.10–12, 102.4–6.

competence. On such assumptions there is no ground whatever to suppose that two reasoners constitute a community *qua* reasoners. What they both exercise is a highly general skill which they may employ without interacting, subscribing to common goals, or doing any of the other things which might be thought necessary or sufficient for the creation of a community or society.

The Stoics, by contrast, are plainly committed to a substantive conception of reason. Just as reason directs the course of the universe as a whole, so it directs individual rational beings in what they should and should not do. Far from being the mere instrument of our passions, if heeded consistently it supplants the passions and replaces the mistaken notion of good and bad implicit in them with the true view. A substantive notion of reason such as this makes it more plausible to think of rational beings as constituting a community in virtue of their rationality. For what they have in common is not just a general skill but an attachment to certain values, namely those prescribed by reason. And common attachment to one rather than another set of values certainly has a strong claim to be considered at least a necessary condition of community, i.e. a requirement that must be satisfied if a plurality of persons is to count as a community. Nonetheless it seems doubtful that it is a sufficient condition. Would we speak of the community of crossword puzzle addicts if the *only* thing they shared was addiction to crossword puzzles, viz. each his or her own private addiction? Probably not.

Does the identification of right reason with law at *Leg.* I 23 and in related texts reflect anything other than that it is *prescriptive* reason that the Stoics are concerned with, and that using the word 'law' is a natural way of talking about authoritative prescription? An important fragment of Chrysippus suggests that there *is* more to the Stoic usage than this. We are told that his work *On law* began as follows (Marcianus *Inst.* I 11.25 = *SVF* III 314):

> Law is King of all things human and divine.
> Law must preside over what is honourable and base, as ruler and as guide, and thus be the standard of what is just and unjust, prescribing to animals whose nature is political what they should do, and prohibiting them from what they should not do.

This text adds to what we know already about the Stoic idea of law as prescriptive reason the information that it is addressed to 'animals whose nature is political'. I take it that Chrysippus means by this expression what Aristotle meant by it: 'animals that are naturally *social*,'[15] or as Arius Didymus puts it at one point in his exposition of Stoic ethics, 'adapted to community' (κοινωνικόν).[16]

The point of the clause is presumably to indicate a specification of the field in which reason makes its prescriptions (cf. also Stob. II 59.4–6). If it is guiding beings who are designed to live in communities, its commands and prohibitions will be concerned with the way they should treat one another as social animals, i.e. as creatures who may have to live with one another. In that case, its designation 'law' is much more strongly motivated than it would be if the only thing in question was simply prescriptive reason without further qualification, addressed as it were to the solitary moral consciousness. For now the idea of regulation of social behaviour turns out after all to be integral to law as understood by the Stoics. This is a conception of law much more closely tied to the well-being of the community than was suggested by our earlier comparison with the voice of conscience and the moral law within. It is still true, of course, that law does not for the Stoa derive its *authority* from society, but what it dictates are principally social or communal norms.

This interpretation of the significance of 'animals whose nature is political' is supported by another feature of the Chrysippus text. The formula 'prescribing to animals whose nature is political what they should do, and prohibiting them from what they should not do' is offered as a gloss on the words 'standard of what is just and unjust'. Those words already make clear that the prescriptive reason with which law is identified is focused on matters of *social* morality: as the Stoics would have conceived it, on treating people

[15] Here I am following the interpretation of Aristotle's notion favoured e.g. by F.D. Miller, 'Aristotle's Political Naturalism', in *Nature, Knowledge and Virtue*: Essays in memory of Joan Kung, edited by T. Penner and R. Kraut (Edmonton 1989) 195–218, at pp. 198–207.

[16] Stob. II 109.17; cf. D.L. VII 123. There is a useful collection of later appearances of the expression in Stoic texts in A. Bonhöffer, *Die Ethik des stoïkers Epictet* (Stuttgart 1894) 118 n. 70, including in Epictetus I 23.1, II 20.6, III 13.5, IV 11.1 (all, interestingly, in dialectical contexts).

as they deserve. For the standard Stoic definition of the virtue justice is 'understanding how to assign to each person what he deserves' (e. g. Stob. II 59.9–10, 84.15–16); and according to Cicero (a little earlier in *Leg.* I, in a similarly Stoic context) *viri doctissimi* derive νόμος, 'law', from νέμω, 'distribute', and connect it with the idea of granting to each his own (I 19).

So the reason which men and gods have in common is not simply prescriptive reason without further qualification. It is prescriptive reason instructing them how to treat each other as social animals. Suppose now three persons *X*, *Y*, *Z* – whether human or divine – each attentive to law so understood. Is there any more cause to reckon *X*, *Y* and *Z* the members of a community just in so far as they are attentive to law than we were able to find with regard to persons having prescriptive reason in general in common? It is true of *X*, *Y* and *Z* not merely that each has an attachment to one and the same set of values, but that each is committed to treating other persons as they deserve, and more generally as persons they have to get on with. Even though none of the three may ever meet or otherwise interact with either of the others, there seem now to be sufficient grounds for describing them as a community, in the same sense as we talk of the community of scholars. A scholar in England and a scholar in Italy may never meet nor exchange ideas or information with one another. But if each is committed not only to dispassionate enquiry but also to an ideal of cooperation with other scholars (including e.g. respect for intellectual property rights, readiness to listen properly to what others have to say, preparedness to learn each other's languages), they may properly be reckoned as belonging to the same community. Of course, if *X* had his own private view, different from the views of *Y* and again of *Z*, as to what treating others as they deserve consists in, then the community they form might turn out to be no community at all – just as scholars who believe in cooperation but hold radically divergent ideas about what constitutes cooperation might not agree on enough to count as a community of scholars. By hypothesis, however, it is reason substantively conceived, and only reason, which dictates the views *X*, *Y* and *Z* all hold on treating others as they deserve. Confronted with the same problems in social ethics, *X*, *Y* and *Z* would reach the same rational, true answer.

The Stoic doctrine that those who have reason, right reason, law and justice in common thereby belong to a single community is therefore a reasonable and intelligible thesis. Is it also reasonable to think of this community as a city? Recall the account of the Stoic idea of a city recorded by Clement:

> A city or a people is something morally good, an organization (σύστημα) or group (πλῆθος) of men administered by law which exhibits refinement.

The moral demands this definition requires a group of human beings to meet if they are to constitute a city are high. Otherwise the conditions it specifies are minimal. Provided a plurality of humans is 'administered by law', they count as citizens of one city. But our specimen persons *X*, *Y* and *Z* satisfy precisely this condition (which of course turns out in their case to be a purely ethical requirement after all, for the law to which they are subject is right reason). It follows that the Stoic idea of a city is nothing but an idea of a community founded on common acceptance of social norms. It is *not* a conception of the *state*: if we take it that there have to be further conditions satisfied (e.g. the centralization of authority, the division of powers) for a community to form a state. The thesis that those who share right reason make up a community is for a Stoic just the same as the thesis that they constitute a city.

Dio's version of the definition of a city provides additionally that it be a group of men living *in the same place*. It is not possible to determine whether this represents the standard Stoic position, nor what connection there might be with Aristotle's discussion of 'living in the same place' in *Pol.* III 3 (especially 1276a24ff.). It may be that it was a question on which different lines were taken in the school, just as different views were held on whether friendship was possible between any two sages whatever or only those who were neighbours acquainted with one another. In any event Dio's residence requirement does not impose any decisive constraint on what communities are cities and what communities are not. For the gods and men who have right reason in common, according to the argument we have been examining, do live in one and the same place, viz. the universe itself, as is spelled out in the next stage of the reasoning.

Where the Stoic definition of the city is inapplicable to them, of course, is in its restriction of citizenship to human beings. It might be conjectured that this is why the sources generally say that the universe is 'as it were' (οἱάνει, ὡσάνει, *quasi*) a city.[17] But though the guess finds support from Dio (*Or.* XXXVI 29), it lacks something in plausibility. It would be odd for the Stoics to enter a scruple about an entirely natural and reasonable extension of 'city' to include divine as well as human citizens. I suspect another motivation for the qualification: homes and cities as ordinarily understood are the creations of men's hands; the universe is the product of nature at work, and so no ordinary home or city – 'as it were' a city, therefore. On this interpretation the qualification makes a concession to a popular assumption which is not shared by the Stoics themselves. All they require of a city (in the relevant sense of the word) is that it be a habitation. How the habitation is constructed is neither here nor there. In that case it would remain true that on their *own* premisses the universe is conceived of as a community, and so as a city – without qualification.

V

In the course of his long exposition in *On Piety* of the attempts made by philosophers to rationalize traditional beliefs about the gods, Philodemus tells us the following at the end of his section on Chrysippus (col. vii 12–viii 4):[18]

> He writes comparable things in *On Nature*, assimilating them to Heraclitus' teachings as well as to those of the poets of which we have spoken. Thus in the first book he says that night is the very first goddess; in the third that the universe of the wise is one, citizenship of it being held by gods and men together,[19] and that war and Zeus are the

[17] See Arius Didymus ap. Euseb. *praep. ev.* XV 15, M. Aurelius IV 3.2, IV 4, Cic. *Fin.* III 64, *ND* II 154.

[18] I cite the text from the recent partial and preliminary edition of A. Henrichs, 'Die Kritik der stoïschen Theologie im PHerc. 1428', *Cron. Erc.* 4 (1974) 5–32. Cf. his earlier article 'Towards a New Edition of Philodemus' Treatise *On piety*', *GRBS* 13 (1972) 67–98.

[19] The Greek reads: ἐν δὲ τῷ τρίτῳ τὸν κ[όσ]μον ἕνα τῶν φρονίμ[ω]ν, συνπολειτευ[ό]μενον θεοῖς καὶ ἀνθρώποις. Henrichs translates: 'Im 3. (Buch), der Kosmos sei einer der Weisen und gehöre zum Staat der Götter und Menschen'. But this misses both the reference to the notion of the cosmic city (συνπολειτευόμενον must therefore be passive, not middle) and the Heraclitean echo (εἷς + gen. is equivalent to εἷς καὶ ὁ αὐτός or κοινός).

> same, as Heraclitus also says; and in the fifth he puts arguments in connection with the thesis that the universe is an animal and rational and exercises understanding[20] and is a god.

Doxography and polemic are never far apart in Philodemus, but there is no reason to suspect distortion or invention here. The doctrine he reports from the first book of *On Nature* is presumably one for which Chrysippus claimed authority in the poets – perhaps Musaeus in particular, for Philodemus has a little before (col. VI 16–26) cited Book II of Chrysippus' *On Gods* for an attempt to syncretize Orpheus, Musaeus, Homer and others with Stoic doctrines, having earlier reported that the verses ascribed to Musaeus make Tartarus or Night the first thing to come into being and the origin of everything else.[21] The appeal to Heraclitus might at first sight appear to be restricted to the thesis about war, since only at that point is his name explicitly invoked. But since *all* these references to *On Nature* are, according to the preamble, introduced to illustrate how Chrysippus exploits Heraclitus as well as the poets, it seems more plausible that *all* the material except the doctrine about night is implied by Philodemus to have been presented by Chrysippus as in harmony with Heraclitean teaching. 'As Heraclitus also says' should probably therefore be taken to relate to the whole of the rest of what is said about the third book, as indicating that we are moving now from poetry to Heraclitus.

There are many sayings Chrysippus might have had in mind in claiming Heraclitean authority for the Stoic doctrine about the universe argued in the fifth book. In the case of the doctrine Philodemus reports from Book III we can be quite specific about the text he must have cited or alluded to (Fr. 53):

> War is the father of all and king of all, and some he shows as gods, others as men; some he makes slaves, others free.

[20] φρονοῦν: Henrichs translates 'zum Denken fähig', but this makes it not dissimilar enough from λογικόν, 'rational'. Once again he misses the Heraclitean echo. The participle is more or less equivalent to φρόνιμον, 'wise'. The verbal form conceivably reflects regard for the point about the difference between the choiceworthy (αἱρετόν) and what-should-be-chosen (αἱρετέον) made at Stob. II 78.7–12 (where φρονεῖν is the example), 97.15–98.13. For discussion of the distinction see A.A. Long and D.N. Sedley, *The Hellenistic Philosophers* (Cambridge 1987) I 202, II 201.

[21] See Text II in Henrichs, *GRBS* 13 (1972) 77–9 (= KRS 18 + 17).

Homer calls Zeus father of gods and men. Heraclitus makes war father of all – gods and men, slaves and free. Chrysippus rightly perceives in the echo of Homer a challenge to Homeric theology, and reasonably enough takes Heraclitus to be identifying Zeus with war, i.e. as offering an account of what Homer's Zeus *really* is.

So much has already been pointed out by editors of Heraclitus.[22] It is arguable that Chrysippus' exploitation of Fr. 53 extends further. Fr. 53 is the only one of Heraclitus' sayings known to us which, while differentiating between them, makes men and gods children and subjects of one and the same father and king.[23] As such it must be the prime candidate for the text Chrysippus drew upon to find in Heraclitus an anticipation of the Stoic idea of a community of men and gods.[24]

[22] So e.g. G.S. Kirk, *Heraclitus: the Cosmic Fragments* (Cambridge 1954) 245–6.

[23] The identity of the gods of whom Heraclitus speaks in this context is of course obscure: for discussion see Kirk, *Heraclitus* 245–9; C.H. Kahn, *The Art and Thought of Heraclitus* (Cambridge 1979) 208–10, 276–8 (cf. also p. 250: 'gods, that is, ... the elements and powers of the cosmos'). There is little evidence in the sources to suggest that in developing the idea of the cosmic city the early Stoics made any greater efforts than Heraclitus to be explicit about the identity of the gods. Perhaps both he and they were more confident that there must *be* divinities (besides the ruling principle of the universe, which does and does not wish to be called Zeus), and that men and gods must share in the same order of things, than of any more specific truths about them. Perhaps, additionally or alternatively, they took the view that in the order of exposition these general truths were more important and fundamental for the doctrine of the cosmos. But at some stage or other in the history of Stoicism, presumably after Chrysippus, the details seem to have been filled in. One pertinent text is a brief remark at the end of Plutarch's treatment of Stoic theology in *de communibus notitiis*, where he refers to the thesis that 'the universe is a city and the stars citizens' (1076 F). He gives the impression that this is a Stoic thesis – but only an impression. There is nothing comparable in other sources which explicitly report Stoic doctrine as such. But there are similar passages, as Cherniss points out *ad loc.*, which it is plausible to take as echoes of Stoic teaching on the cosmic city, notably Philo, *de spec. leg.* I 13–14, Manilius V 734–5. The theory of the cosmic city is here married with the polytheism built into Stoic cosmology, and in particular with the doctrine that 'sun and moon and other gods that have a similar account' are perishable divine beings (Plu. *Stoic. rep.* 1052 A; cf. *Comm. not.* 1074 D–1075 D).

[24] For more on Chrysippus' treatment of Fr. 53 see p. 89 below. One would expect Fr. 114 to have been exploited in this connection, for it compares the reliance which those who speak with understanding should have on what is common to the faith a city has in its law. But there is no definite indication of this in our *testimonia* relating to *On Nature*, although Fr. 114 was certainly heavily exploited in Cleanthes' *Hymn to Zeus* (especially lines 24–5) and in the Stoic

Fr. 53 will not support Chrysippus' further thesis that the universe is one, common to the wise (φρόνιμοι). Here the best candidates for the Heraclitean texts he relies upon appear to be Fr. 2:

> Although the *logos* is common the many live as though they had a private understanding (φρόνησις).

and Fr. 31 (ad init.):

> This universe, the same for all,[25] did none of gods or men make.

Heraclitus implies that only those with true understanding (i.e. the φρόνιμοι) will realize that the *logos* of the universe is a single principle, making it one ordering of things for all. If Chrysippus' thesis that 'the universe is one, [common] to the wise' (τὸν κόσμον ἕνα τῶν φρονίμων) goes beyond this, it is only in depriving the many of a share in the universe they do not comprehend – although Heraclitus would scarcely have objected to the consequence that each of the many lives in his own pseudo-world.

The implication of Philodemus' testimony, that according to the Stoics only the wise exercise true citizenship of the universe, is supported both by other evidence on the point and by further information on the contents of Chrysippus' *On Nature*.

Dio's *Or.* XXXVI supplies the most nuanced account.[26] We noted

doctrine of providence, where it is echoed in Plutarch's report (*de Iside* 369 A) that they recognize ἕνα λόγον καὶ μίαν πρόνοιαν... περιγιγνομένην ἁπάντων καὶ κρατοῦσαν (cf. Kirk, *Heraclitus* 49–50).

[25] *Contra* Kirk (*Heraclitus* 307–10; cf. KRS p. 198 n. 1), I incline to the view that the words τὸν αὐτὸν ἁπάντων are authentically Heraclitean (with e.g. Kahn, *The Art and Thought of Heraclitus* 312 n. 121).

[26] But it is worth mentioning Philo's interpretation, if only to notice how he uses this construction of the Stoic doctrine for his own purposes. At *op. mund.* 3 (cf. *Mos.* I 157, II 50) he says: 'The law-abiding man is on that account a citizen of the universe (κοσμοπολίτης), regulating his actions in line with the will of nature, in accordance with which the universe as a whole is administered.' Elsewhere he is prepared to restrict cosmic citizenship even further (*Cherub.* 120–1): 'Each of us has come into this universe as into a foreign city, in which before birth we had no share, and on arrival takes lodgings, until he exhausts the appointed time of life... God alone strictly speaking is a citizen, and everything that is created is a lodger and an alien: so-called citizens are spoken of as such by popular use of the word rather than in truth. It is a sufficient gift for wise men if, when ranked against God the only citizen, they receive the rank of aliens and lodgers, since none of the fools becomes an alien or lodger in the city of god at all, but is discovered as nothing more than a fugitive.'

that in his discussion of Phocylides' saying about Nineveh (in the course of his elaboration of the consequences of the Stoic definition of city), Dio argued that what is not law-abiding is not properly a city. This led him to wonder whether any city which does not consist entirely of good men is a law-abiding city. Without committing himself to an answer on that issue he does assert that a *good* city can consist only of members who are all good (§§20–2). What of the cosmic city? Dio is sure that *that* must be a good or 'purely happy' city. He says (§23):

> This is the only constitution or indeed city one should call purely happy: the community of gods with one another – even if you include also everything that is capable of reason, counting in men with gods, as children are said to partake in the city along with men, being naturally citizens, not because they understand and perform the duties of citizens nor because they share in the law, being without comprehension of it.

Dio obviously has in mind here the definition of the universe as an organization of gods and men and so as a city; and the reference to 'everything that is capable of reason' (ξύμπαν τό λογικόν) suggests that he is also thinking of the argument for the cosmic city thesis preserved by Cicero, and alluded to by himself a little later (§31). He is evidently tackling a problem for the definition: given that men in general are *not* morally good, how can they be members of the cosmic city without destroying its happiness and goodness or even its status as a city? Dio's solution is to see men as not full but potential citizens, like children. The solution is probably the orthodox Stoic position, for as well as exploiting the definition of man as by nature a political animal (NB 'being naturally citizens') and as such the recipient of the prescriptions and prohibitions of law or right reason, Dio ends with words ('nor because they share in the law, being without comprehension (ἀξύνετοι) of it') which have the tell-tale Heraclitean ring we have now learned to associate with Chrysippus. Here besides Fr. 2 it is the famous first sentence of Heraclitus' book that is being echoed (Fr. 1):

> Of this *logos* which is always men that prove to be without comprehension (ἀξύνετοι), both before they have heard it and when once they have heard it.

Heraclitean allusion appears to have saturated Chrysippus' *On Nature*, the work which is Philodemus' source for the doctrine of the cosmic city. We are relatively well informed about this treatise, mostly because Plutarch frequently quotes or makes précis from it in his tract on Stoic self-contradictions.[27] From Book I he cites the following (*Stoic. rep.* 1053 A):

> The transformation of fire is like this: by way of air it turns into water; and from this, as earth is precipitated, air evaporates; and as the air is subtilized, ether is diffused in a circle, and the stars along with the sun are kindled from the sea.

This is no more than a rewriting of the key Heraclitean text whose first half is preserved in Fr. 31, and which is paraphrased at D.L. IX 9–10. Also in *Stoic. rep.* (1049 AB) Plutarch introduces a sequence of quotations on the conformity of all that happens with 'common nature and its *logos*' with an allusion to Heraclitus' memorable image of the barley-drink (Fr. 125):

> Having first of all in the first book of *On Nature* compared the everlasting nature of change with the barley-drink, twirling and disturbing in different ways the different things that come to be, he says this: 'Since the management of the wholes proceeds in this way, it is necessarily in conformity with it that we are in whatever state we may be, whether –

[27] Von Arnim raises the question (*SVF* III p. 204) whether *On Nature* is the same work as is elsewhere referred to as *Physics* (τὰ φυσικά). Some at least of the doctrines attributed to *Physics* are unlikely to have been advanced in a cosmological work such as *On Nature* plainly was. Thus D.L. VII 50, 55, 157 (all relating to Book II of *Physics*) are concerned with what one might call the physics of psychology (and VII 158, also a reference to Book II, is naturally taken in the same way). D.L. VII 151, relating to Book III, is concerned with the doctrine of total mixture: it seems highly unlikely that *On Nature* III said anything on this topic, to judge from our information about it. The references to *Physics* I (D.L. VII 134, 136, 142) deal with matters (the active and passive principles, the four elements and their transformations) which do correspond well with what we know of *On Nature* I. But (1) the references to *Physics* II and III have clearly suggested a distinct work; (2) all the information about what is called *Physics*, and none of that about what is called *On Nature*, comes in Diogenes Laertius – who cannot be presumed to have any specific information about the latter work; (3) there is no reason why Chrysippus should not have discussed some topics in at least two distinct works: *Physics* I and *On Nature* I. It is overwhelmingly probable, therefore, that the titles are *not* alternative designations of a single treatise.

> contrary to our individual nature – we are ill or maimed or have become grammarians or musicians.'

This gives some indication of how Chrysippus must have spelled out the Heraclitean idea that war is king and father of all, i.e. that the cosmic order is a function of change and conflict. The only quotation from Book II (*Stoic. rep.* 1050 EF) finds Chrysippus developing the same general theme, concerned as it is with the place of vice in the providential scheme of nature.

More relevant to our immediate concerns, however, are the three extracts Plutarch preserves from Book III, for this is the book which contained the account of the cosmic city:

1 A text cited to illustrate the Stoic view that there are no degrees of virtue or vice (*Stoic. rep.* 1038 CD):

> He says in the third book *On Nature*: 'As it befits Zeus to glory in himself and his way of life and to be haughty and, if one should put it this way, to carry his head high and plume himself and boast, since he lives in a way worth boasting about, so does this befit all good men, since they are not surpassed in anything by Zeus'.

2 From *Stoic. rep.* 1048 B:

> In the third book *On Nature* he says that some men are felicitated on being kings and being wealthy as if they were being felicitated for using golden chamber-pots and wearing golden tassels, but that to the good man losing his fortune is like losing a drachma, and falling ill is like stumbling.

3 From *Stoic. rep.* 1042 AB:

> He declares that vice is the essence of unhappiness, in every book on physics and ethics writing and contending that living in accordance with vice is the same as living unhappily. But in the third book *On Nature*, after first remarking that it is profitable to live a fool rather than not to live a life even if one is never going to be wise, he adds: 'For to human beings good things are such that in a way even evils have the advantage over intermediates.'

Chrysippus went on to say, probably immediately (*Stoic. rep.* 1042 C; cf. *Comm. not.* 1064 E):

> But it is not these that have the advantage, but reason; and it is incumbent upon us rather to live a life with reason, even if we are to be fools.

It is not possible to reconstruct the context or contexts of argument in which these passages in Chrysippus' Book III occurred, but some inferences appear to be in order. First, (2) and (3) together suggest that Chrysippus was intent on drawing a contrast between the attitudes towards indifferents appropriate to the good man and the fool; and (3) that he employed the Heraclitean language of φρονεῖν etc. in talking of folly and wisdom, confirming what Philodemus had already indicated in this connection. The division of men into good and bad, wise and fools, in a treatise of the kind we have glimpsed in Plutarch's quotations, calls Cleanthes' intensely Heraclitean *Hymn to Zeus* strongly to mind.[28] Cleanthes begins the second main section of his poem (ll.7–31) with an account of the physical universe (specially emphasizing fire) and its ordering (ll.7–14); stresses that nothing that happens happens apart from Zeus – except for evil, which even so has a place in the providential scheme of things (ll.15–21); and concludes with a diagnosis of the condition of the wicked (ll.22–31). Chrysippus' plan of campaign looks to have been very similar: Book I containing an account of the physical universe focusing on the role of fire, but going on to argue that everything that happens happens in conformity with common nature and its *logos* (and incidentally praising Homer's saying (*Iliad* A5) 'the will of Zeus was being accomplished', ap. Plu. *Stoic. rep.* 1050 B); Book II discussing the providential role of vice; and Book III exploring the nature of the division between the good and the wicked – all with a pregnancy of Heraclitean reference no less emphatic than Cleanthes'. The conjecture that in their different ways the *Hymn to Zeus* and *On Nature* sought to develop an original Zenonian treatment of these themes seems irresistible.[29]

[28] On the Heraclitean dimension of the *Hymn to Zeus* see especially A.A. Long, 'Heraclitus and Stoicism', ΦΙΛΟΣΟΦΙΑ 5–6 (1975–6) 133–56; the most important echoes are noted in N. Hopkinson (ed.), *A Hellenistic Anthology* (Cambridge 1988) 132–6.

[29] I do not dissent from Long' s view (ΦΙΛΟΣΟΦΙΑ 5–6 (1975–6) 133–56) that it was Cleanthes who was mainly responsible for developing the Heraclitean 'anticipations' of Stoicism. But (as Long allows, *ibld.* p. 152) his impetus in this direction was 'probably stimulated by Zeno' himself, for it was worked out so extensively and determinedly that it must have claimed Zenonian au-

Second, the evidence of (2) and (3) fits well with Philodemus' implication that true citizenship of the cosmic city was restricted to the good and wise. Does (1) throw further light on this thesis? Its main point, of course, is to stress in the most provocative way conceivable that a good man is in no way inferior to Zeus, putting the kinship of man and god in egalitarian terms never contemplated by Cleanthes in his treatment of the theme in the *Hymn* (ll.4–5). Nonetheless it has an obvious bearing on the notion of the community of men and gods; and whether in *On Nature* or elsewhere Chrysippus appears to have spelled out at least one consequence relevant to the notion (*Comm. not.* 1076 A):

> Zeus does not excel Dion in virtue, and Dion and Zeus, being wise, are benefited alike by each other, when the one encounters a movement of the other. For this and nothing else is the good that comes to men from gods and gods from men, once these have become wise.

Plutarch goes on to object (*ibid.* 1076 B):

> This wise man exists nowhere on earth, nor ever has existed, but there are countless myriads of men at the extremity of unhappiness under that political government (πολίτεια) or rule of Zeus which provides the best administration (διοίκησις).

Perhaps we may infer that any good man has as strong a claim to citizenship of the cosmic community as its ruler Zeus himself.

In the cosmic city argument examined above in Section III other things are said to have been created for the sake of men and

thority, nor would Chrysippus have continued the project otherwise (as the evidence of *On Nature* shows he did with more enthusiasm than Long concedes, *ibid.* pp. 152–3). In general Chrysippus accords Cleanthes no special respect (cf. D.L. VII 179), but both take it as their duty to explicate Zeno's doubtless often pregnant but pithy statements, and many of their disputes are apparently *inter alia* arguments about Zenonian exegesis. This is true e.g. of their differing accounts of the τέλος (D.L. VII 87–9) and of φαντασία (Sextus *M* VII 227–31), and may be suspected of being so with regard to other topics too, as on τέχνη (see J. Mansfeld, '*Techne*: A New Fragment of Chrysippus', *GRBS* 24 (1983) 57–65) and ἀπόδειξις (see the celebrated paper of J. Brunschwig, 'Proof Defined', in *Doubt and Dogmatism*, ed. M. Schofield, M. Burnyeat, J. Barnes (Oxford 1980) 125–60). Cf. D.N. Sedley, 'Philosophical Allegiance in the Greco-Roman World', in *Philosophia Togata*, ed. M. Griffin and J. Barnes (Oxford 1989) 97–119.

gods. One and perhaps both of Plutarch's remaining quotations from *On Nature* bear on this thesis. At *Stoic. rep.* 1044 D:

> In the fifth book *On Nature*, after saying that bugs are useful in waking us up and mice in making us attentive about putting things away carefully, and that it is probable that nature loves the beautiful, since she delights in diversity, he says this *verbatim*: 'The tail of the peacock would be an especially impressive manifestation of this. For here nature makes it clear that the creature has come into being for the sake of the tail and not *vice versa*, and the male having come into being for this reason, it followed that there must be a female.'

Nature's production of animals to provide a beautiful spectacle is evidently taken to be no less evidence of the anthropocentric focus of creation than its supply of mice and bugs. Plutarch's other reference to Book v follows in his next chapter (*Stoic. rep.* 1045 A):

> In the fifth book (again) *On Nature* he says that Hesiod did well to prohibit urinating into rivers and springs, but that there is still more reason to refrain from urinating against an altar or shrine of a god. For it is not to the point if dogs and asses and little children do it, since they are without any regard or understanding for such matters.

The original point of this remark of Chrysippus is obscure. Conceivably he was emphasizing our kinship with the gods and commensurately the great gulf fixed between us and the irrational animals.

No doubt Chrysippus developed the doctrine of the cosmic city in more than one of his works. If the argument of Section III above is correct, it is likely to have figured prominently in *On Providence*, and it is probable also that that version was the original from which Cicero's account in *ND* II 154 and Arius Didymus apud Euseb. *praep. ev.* XV 15 ultimately derive.[30] But the argument of the present section suggests that it figured no less prominently in the Heraclitean *On Nature*, and that this version may have been known to Dio, since he seems to echo its Heraclitean vocabu-

[30] The cosmic city argument is the first argument in the fourth section of *ND*. This may reflect the importance assigned to it by Chrysippus himself.

lary and to pursue the issue of the moral and intellectual virtue of the members of the cosmic city in a way which recalls *On Nature* but is not taken up in the doxographical reports we studied in Sections III and IV.

VI

It is one thing to make the universe the *location* of a community or city of gods and men, and so itself a city in sense (a), habitation. It is another, as Arius Didymus implies (apud Euseb. *praep. ev.* xv 15), to conceive of it as a city in the sense (b) of an *organization* or group of gods and men. To move from (a) to (b) in talk of a cosmic city is an easy and harmless step, if construed as comparable to the step we take if we move from speaking of Athens as the place where the Athenians live to meaning by 'Athens' just 'the Athenians'. In Cicero's version of the argument studied in Section III the universe is clearly conceived of as a city in sense (a). But when Arius Didymus indicates that we can also talk of it as a city in sense (b), the obvious reason is simply that it gets so called after the community which inhabits it. Certainly there is no evidence in the material considered in Sections III–V, including the extracts cited from Chrysippus' *On Nature*, to suggest any other interpretation.

In Dio's *logos Borysthenitikos*, however, version (b) of the doctrine of the cosmic city is construed in a more direct way. It is as though the buildings and the town plan of Athens were called an organization of human beings – or rather, said to be *like* an organization of human beings – in virtue *not* of the men who live there but because of the way the buildings and town plan are themselves organized. On this interpretation of the cosmic city, the universe is said to be a city because of its *own* plan: on account not of what it contains but of what it is in itself. That plan is 'as it were' a city – i.e. analogous to a human organization. More specifically, Dio claims that the universe is organized as though it were administered by a king.

A direct analogy between city and cosmos such as this *cannot* be inferred from the thesis that the cosmos is the habitation of all rational beings. For that thesis implies nothing about the intrinsic character of the universe. Nor from the premiss that the universe is organized like the administration of a king can one derive without further assumptions the conclusion that it is the habitation of a community of men and gods. In short, Dio's analogy appears to constitute a completely different theory from that represented by the canonical reading of the cosmic city doctrine found in Chrysippus and subsequently in the doxographical tradition.

His account of the cosmic city runs from §§29–38. He begins with an introduction which insists emphatically on the analogical status of the idea of the cosmic city (§§29–30). We shall return to this introduction in due course, but for the present we move on to the summary he next offers of the point of the doctrine (§31):

> This theory (λόγος) in brief, aims to harmonize the human race with the divine, and to embrace anything capable of reason (λογικόν) in a single account (λόγος), finding this the only strong and indissoluble principle of community and justice.

This is clear evidence that Dio knows what I am calling the canonical reading of the doctrine: his summary contains the same ideas as sustain the key move in the relevant texts of Arius Didymus (see Section III) and Cicero's *de legibus* (see Section IV); and his talk of harmonizing 'the human race with the divine' recalls the moral Cicero extracts from his argument in the immediate context in *de legibus* I 22–4. But the lion's share of his discussion (§§31–7) is taken up with his development of the direct analogy between city and cosmos, which he offers in *support* of the canonical thesis he has summarized. (The first sentence of the development begins: '*For* indeed it is in line with this [κατά τοῦτο; sc. harmony] that the word "city" should be used.') Only when Dio rounds things off at the end of the whole section does he return to canonical material (§38):

> This, then, is the theory of the philosophers, which establishes a good community, well disposed to men (φιλάνθρωπον), of gods and men, giving a share of law and constitution not to any living being whatsoever, but to those who have a share in reason and wisdom (φρόνησις).

Is this how an orthodox early Stoic would have argued? The proportions of Dio's discussion and the role he gives to the direct analogy may well make us suspect not. Such suspicions are confirmed when we examine the details of the text. It contains a main and a subsidiary argument for the comparison of the universe to a city. To begin with I concentrate on the main argument (§§31–2).

Dio informs us that a city rightly so called does *not* (i) have mean or morally wicked leaders, *nor* (ii) is it torn apart and in continual στάσις because of tyranny, democracy, oligarchy and 'other such sicknesses (ἀρρωστήματα)'. Rather

> (i') it is adorned with the best and most temperate kingship, (ii') being in truth governed as a kingship in accordance with law, in complete friendship and concord. (§32) It is precisely this [sc. kingship] which the wisest and most senior ruler and law-giver prescribes (προστάττει) for all, mortal and immortal, the leader of this universe as a whole and the master of the whole of being. In this way [sc. by his leadership and mastery] he himself expounds and provides his own administration (διοίκησις) as a pattern (παράδειγμα) of the happy and blessed condition [sc. kingship]. And the divine poets, learning from the Muses, hymn him and name him 'father of gods and men'.

The relevance of this train of thought to the community of men and gods is not very clear. Presumably the point is that only kingship can secure friendship and concord among the members of a community; and friendship and concord are necessary if harmony is to be achieved. By hypothesis the community of men and gods is harmonious. Therefore it must be administered as a kingship.

If this is what Dio is suggesting, he is not convincing. On the canonical Stoic theory, even as his own summaries of it imply, it is right reason which makes of men and gods not merely a community but a good community. Only if kingship is taken as a mere metaphor for the directive efficacy of right reason, as in Chrysippus' dictum that law is king of all things human and divine, does the theory make harmony depend on kingship. But Dio is evidently thinking of kingship here as a specific form of constitution.

Nor is this the only feature of the passage which is not Stoic, or at any rate not purely Stoic. Its style is Platonic in aspiration, and no doubt designed to advance the syncretism of the Stoic and the Platonic which is a principal object of the speech as a whole. As to diction, the list of imperfect constitutions recalls Plato, but their description as 'sicknesses' (ἀρρωστήματα) exploits a well-known and distinctive term in the vocabulary of Stoic moral vocabulary. The early Stoics called Zeus 'leader of this administration (διοίκησις) of things' (D.L. VII 87), but the immediate source of the phrase 'leader of this οὐρανός' as applied to him is the *Phaedrus* (246 E), as the reader is by now trained to notice. What is not Stoic at all is the syllogism Dio is effectively proposing:

1 If and only if something is administered as a kingship, is it a city properly so called.
2 But the universe is administered as if it were a kingship.
3 Therefore the universe is as it were a city properly so called.

There is no good reason to suppose that the early Stoics considered kingship the only or the best constitution.

Plato, of course, is the most famous proponent in antiquity of premiss (1) or at any rate of kingship as the best constitution. But the appearance here not only of (1) but of the idea that kingship is the constitution modelled on Zeus's rule over the universe, and indeed the extended treatment of divine kingship in this context, are to be explained by Dio's own considerable preoccupation with kingship, attested most notably by the four *logoi* on the subject which are generally placed at the beginning of his corpus. The passage most relevant to *Or.* XXXVI 31–2 is the section of *Or.* III (42–50) where Dio argues for the position he wishes to take in constitutional theory. He develops his entirely conventional views in language steeped in allusions to the philosophical tradition within the conventional Aristotelian framework of three good and three deviant constitutions.[31] Of the good forms democracy is declared to be virtually impossible, and aristocracy further from possibility and expediency than when 'the city or a number of peoples or all mankind is well administered by the judgment and

[31] Cf. H. von Arnim, *Leben und Werke des Dio von Prusa*, 419.

virtue of one good man' (§45), or, as he put it at §50 in a phrase which anticipates XXXVI 32,[32] 'the happy and divine condition which now prevails'. He goes on (§50):

> Now there are many clear images and patterns (παραδείγματα) not obscure of this form of rule, since in herds and swarms nature indicates that it is natural for the stronger to exercise rule over the weaker and forethought for them. However there could be no more obvious or beautiful [pattern] than the leadership of the whole which occurs under the first and best god.

Scholars sometimes talk of Cynic or Stoic influence on Dio's conception of kingship. But the comparison of earthly and divine kings was a commonplace (cf. e.g. Isoc. *Nic.* 25–6, Sen. *clem.* I 7, Plu. *ad princ. inerud.* 780 E–781 C, Clem. *Strom.* I 24); and although 'leadership of the whole' is characteristically Stoic talk, we have already noted its Platonic antecedents. Above all, there is no hint anywhere in *Or.* III 42–50[33] of the doctrine of the cosmic city. The natural inference is that in *Or.* XXXVI 31–32 Dio has attempted to force a marriage between Platonic – Aristotelian kingship theory and the Stoic idea of the community of gods and men which has the cosmos as its home. The attempt fails.

At the end of XXXVI 32 Dio supports his view that 'the master of the whole of being' provides his own administration of things as a pattern or paradigm for us by an appeal to the poets' designation of Zeus as 'father of gods and men'. Gearing his discourse to the tastes of his Borysthenean audience again, he devotes the rest of his treatment of the cosmic city analogy to the poets and to this *endoxon*. From it, however, he extracts a further proof of the analogy. I quote the relevant section (§§35–7):

> In fact all these poets in the same way call the first and greatest god 'father' of the whole race of rational beings

[32] Noted by von Arnim, *ibid.* 485.

[33] I should stress that it is with regard to this section of *Or.* III only (i.e. the relevant passage for considering *Or.* XXXVI 31–2) that I am presently denying significant Stoic or Cynic influence, which has in any case been detected rather in the earlier and later sections of the speech where Dio explains what a king is and should be. See e.g. R. Höistad, *Cynic Hero and Cynic King* (Lund 1948) 183–94.

> taken together – and 'king' too. Trusting them men erect altars to Zeus the king, and what is more some do not hesitate to address him as father in their prayers, on the assumption that there is rule and organization of the universe of this sort. So on this basis I think they would not hesitate to declare the whole universe the house of Zeus, since he is father of the beings within it, and – by Zeus! – his city, as we [sc. we philosophers] do in our analogy, in virtue of his more important rule. For 'kingship' would be more appropriately applied to a city than a house. For surely those who call him who is over the wholes 'king' would not refuse to agree that the whole is governed as a kingdom. And if they say that it is governed as a kingdom they would not deny that it is governed politically, nor that there is political government of the universe. But if they concede 'political government' they would not be put off from agreeing 'city' or something with a political form of government very like it.

The chain of inferences at the end of this passage is certainly Stoic in manner. Is Dio reproducing a genuine stretch of early Stoic argument? It would not be beyond his powers as a stylist to produce something of his own in Stoic idiom, just as he can imitate Platonic ὕψος. On the other hand our discussion of Chrysippus' use of Heraclitus Fr. 53 in *On Nature* suggests an inference on *his* part from the idea of Zeus as king to the thesis that the gods and men referred to by Heraclitus are fellow-*citizens*. Dio's argument is exactly the sort of argument needed to make the inference plausible; and we have seen evidence that Dio is aware of the Heraclitean dimension of the cosmic city doctrine, perhaps because he knew *On Nature*. I therefore conjecture Chrysippean authorship,[34] and indeed a further 'fragment' of *On Nature*. It is true that in the early part of the passage Dio talks about the organization of the universe in connection with kingship as he had in the unStoic §§31–2. But it is not this (as it was in §§31–2) which supports the inference to a cosmic city. More important is the

[34] Like §§20 [*SVF* III 329], 23 [*SVF* III 334], and 29 [*SVF* II 1130], von Arnim includes §37 [*SVF* III 1129] in his collection of early Stoic *testimonia*, albeit in his lowest grade of typography, indicating merely 'quae aliquo modo ad cognoscendam Chrysippi doctrinam utilia viderentur' (Vol. I p. v).

initial talk of Zeus as 'king' of 'the whole race of rational beings taken together'.

In his introductory remarks on the cosmic city doctrine construed as analogy (§§29–30), Dio gives an indication of the Stoic arguments which seem to have encouraged him to take it in what I am arguing to be the unStoic way he does (§30):

> But they make a sort of *comparison* of the present ordering [sc. of the universe] – when the whole has been separated and divided into many forms of plants and living beings mortal and immortal, and again of air and earth and water and fire, being nonetheless one thing by nature in all these and governed by one soul and power – with a city: (i) on account of the multitude of things which come into and out of being within it, and again (ἔτι) (ii) because of the arrangement and orderliness of the administration.

Fortunately there is evidence in Stoic sources relating to both (i) and (ii). They show clearly enough that, while Dio is right to see the Stoics as making analogical use of the idea of the city in discussions of the universe, they do not support his own interpretation of the cosmic city doctrine.

For (ii) we have a doxographical notice from Aristocles preserved by Eusebius (*praep. ev.* XV 14.2):

> Next, they say also that the universe as a whole is consumed by fire at certain times determined by fate, and then once more reconstituted as an order of things. But the primal fire is as it were a seed, containing the formulae of all things and the causes of what has come into being, what is coming into being, and what will be. The nexus and consequentiality of these is fate, knowledge, truth, and a law governing the things that are which is inevitable and inescapable. In this way the condition of the universe is administered (διοικεῖται) superlatively well, as in a political society (πολιτεία) with excellent laws.

To be sure, Aristocles' Stoics make the political comparison with respect to the cosmic cycle, Dio's with respect to the present διακόσμησις. But the function of the comparison was no doubt the same: to supply passing imaginative enhancement of our sense of the organization of the cosmos – not to advance a doctrine, let alone the canonical doctrine of the cosmic city.

The Stoic teaching to which (i) refers is preserved in Epictetus, who attributes it to 'the philosophers' (*Diss.* III 24.10–12):

> This universe is a single city, and the substance out of which it has been fashioned is one. And it is necessary that there is a certain periodic change and a giving place of one thing to another, and that some things are dissolved and others come into being, some remain in the same place and others are moved. And all things are full of friends, first of gods, then also of men who have been made naturally akin to each other. And some of them must be with each other, others must depart; and they must rejoice in those who are with them, but not grieve at those who depart. And man, in addition to being by nature high-minded and capable of despising all things outside the scope of his purpose, possesses also this further property, of not being rooted in the earth nor of growing attached to it, but of moving now to one place and now to another, at one time under the pressure of certain needs and at another just for the sake of the spectacle.

The necessity of birth and death is what Aristotle would have called a hypothetical necessity, dictated by the providential economy of the universe. Epictetus brings the point out vividly elsewhere (*Diss.* IV 1.106):

> Make room for others. Others too must be born as you too were born, and once born they must have room and housing – the essential requisites. But if the first-comers do not move out, what is left for them? Why are you insatiate? Why never satisfied? Why do you crowd the universe?

In these texts Epictetus argues *from*, not to, the conception of the universe as a well-ordered city. He does not hedge his reference to it with an 'as it were'. But the force of what he has to say turns on analogy: 'Think of the pattern of life and death as if it were the movement of human beings into and out of a city. Remember in particular that people do and should leave the city for proper and intelligible reasons which justify neither reluctance on the part of the agents not grief on the part of others.' This is indeed the cosmic city, but conceived in the standard way as the *habitation* of rational beings:[35] who themselves constitute a community – and, as the Stoics elsewhere say, a city – in an altogether un-analogical sense.

[35] It is worth noting (and not surprising) that when our sources talk of the cosmic city in the sense 'habitation' they are often ready to speak of the universe indifferently as a city *or* house/home (e.g. Cic. *ND* II 154, with many further references in Pease's note; cf. also D.T. Runia, *Philo of Alexandria and the Timaeus of Plato* (Leiden 1986) 165–9 with nn. 30–2). In so doing they effect at least the beginnings of an assimilation of the Stoic doctrine with the famous Aristotelian analogy (Cic. *ND* II 95).

4

From republicanism to natural law

I

Seneca writes as follows (*de otio* 4):

> Let us embrace with our minds two commonwealths (*res publicae*): one great and truly common – in which gods and men are contained, in which we look not to this or that corner, but measure the bounds of our state (*civitas*) with the sun; the other the one to which the particular circumstances of birth have assigned us – this will be the commonwealth of the Athenians or the Carthaginians or some other city (*urbs*) which pertains not to all men but a particular group of them (*certos*). Some give service to both commonwealths at the same time – the greater and the lesser; some only to the lesser, some only to the greater. This greater commonwealth we are able to serve even in leisure, or rather perhaps better in leisure – so that we may enquire what virtue is, whether it is one or many, whether nature or art makes men good; whether this world, which embraces seas and lands and things grafted on to sea and lands, is unique, or whether God has scattered many bodies of this sort; etc.

For Seneca the true city is the cosmic city. So it was for the other leading Stoic authors of the early Empire: Musonius Rufus, Epictetus, Marcus Aurelius; as also for Philo Judaeus and Dio Chrysostom. We have noted traces of it in Manilius and Plutarch, who again appear to know no other Stoic idea of the true city. None of these texts is doxographical in character. But the few doxographical items which bear directly on the topic say nothing different. According to Clement it is the universe which the Stoics identify as the true city, and Cicero consistently represents this and this alone as the Stoic position. Nowhere in all this material is there any hint of Zeno's Spartan republic of sages. Plutarch in *de Alex. virt.* of course refers to Zeno and his *Republic*, but assimilates the contents of the work to something resembling the doctrine of the cosmic city.

One might be tempted to conclude that Zeno's *Republic* not only embarrassed later Stoics but had little influence upon them. It propounded a conception of the true city which may have stimulated his immediate associates to intense interest in love and in Sparta, but was apparently abandoned in the later Stoic and Stoicizing tradition. Indeed it seems something of a fluke that any specific reports about its distinctive political ideal survive at all. We have scraps of doxographical information in D.L. VII about love and about the holding of women in common (attributed also to Chrysippus' *On the Republic*), and some misinformation about marriage. On the key points, however, just two unlikely non-Stoic sources rescue us from total ignorance: the magpie curiosity of Athenaeus, and the obscure saga of censorship and criticism associated by Diogenes Laertius with the names of Athenodorus, Cassius and Isidorus. The Zeno disclosed in these texts may well appear to be a Zeno unassimilated by Stoic orthodoxy or by writers dependent in one way or another on Stoic doctrine. They are very specifically about Zeno, not about any more generally Stoic positions.

II

It would be remarkable if the *Republic* had indeed had as little effect on later Stoicism as the train of thought entertained in Section I suggests. In general Zeno's ideas and indeed his *ipsissima verba* were conceived as defining what Stoicism was, at any rate in the Hellenistic period. They were treated as the starting points for the theoretical elaborations which filled the treatises of Cleanthes and especially Chrysippus, and were in consequence indirectly, as well as occasionally directly, absorbed by later Stoicism. Nor would it have been easy for Stoics subsequent to Zeno to treat the *Republic* as a minor work, which need not therefore be exploited to the full. If the arguments of Chapter 2 of this book are on the right lines, it was conceived as a major philosophical statement challenging comparison with Plato's *Republic*.

I shall argue that Zeno's *Republic* in fact had an enormous influence on Stoicism, and that we should not be misled into thinking otherwise by the apparent neglect of its specific proposals about the ideal city.

Most fundamental and far-reaching from the point of view of later Stoicism was Zeno's identification of the wise or morally good man as the only true citizen, friend and free person, and the bad man as alien, enemy and slave. Its effect within Stoicism was pervasive. Consider for example the third principal division of Stobaeus' account of Arius Didymus' presentation of Stoic ethics (S3 hereafter). S3 is entirely devoted to discussion of the morally good and the morally bad man, as is made clear early in the main part of the discussion (II 99.3–5):

> Zeno and the Stoic philosophers who give him their allegiance hold that there are two classes of men: the morally good and the morally bad.

Its sequel is an elaborate explanation of the properties of the two classes, and especially of a huge range of contrary predicates which divide them. They naturally include *rich*, *poor*, *free*, *slave* (II 101.14–20), which figure famously in Stoic paradoxes about the sage widely quoted in Greek and Latin literature as well as philosophy, but also whole batteries of attributes less familiar as Stoic, e.g. (of the good man) *mild*, *quiet*, *orderly* (II 115.10–17), or again *canny*, *good at hitting the aim*, *good at seeing the right moment*, *quick to see what is appropriate*, *artless*, *uncomplicated*, *straightforward*, *unaffected* (II 108.9–11). A sequence of particular interest from our point of view is: *having the skill to be a king*, *a general*, *a politician*, *a householder and an acquirer of property* (II 100.4–6). In the case of most of these 'political' predicates (if not with some of the others just mentioned) the text somewhere or other supplies some justification for attributing the properties in question to the sage. Thus, even if he is not in a position to exercise his skill, only the wise man is capable of the supervision appropriate for ruling people and its species, which include that required in a king and again in a general (II 102.11–15). Similarly, only the morally good man knows from what sources one should acquire property and when and how and to what extent (II 95.14–19, 21–3). Another body of material in S3 which is of immediate relevance to our concerns is the treatment of law and the city examined in Appendixes F and G. This is where Arius Didymus explains why the morally bad man is an *exile, boorish, wild, savage, tyrannical* and *ungrateful*, because he is *not law-abiding* (II 103.9–104.9); and also why he is *without honour*, because he is not worthy of the respect that is the prize for virtue which benefits others, having no share in that virtue (II 103.4–8).

The vast range of predicates attributed in Arius Didymus to the good and the bad man respectively evidently expands far beyond the items picked out by Zeno in the *Republic* and no doubt subsequently in other writings, even assuming (as is reasonable) that Zeno's list was longer than any of our sources explicitly attests. Here is a classic instance of the scholastic elaboration of a Zenonian idea by Chrysippus and the subsequent school tradition. For evidence I have turned to Arius Didymus. But it would have been possible to cite as well or instead Cicero, Plutarch, Sextus, Diogenes Laertius, Alexander of Aphrodisias, Seneca and even Horace.

In Arius Didymus as in many of the other sources it is clear that there has been not merely expansion but a degree of reorientation of Zeno's treatment of the good and the bad man. The *Republic* was a work of political philosophy, albeit directed (like all ancient political philosophy) by ethical concerns, and although radical in its implied attack on existing forms of society. Its account of the good and the bad man was presumably conceived as an answer to the question of the nature of the citizen body and its relation to kinship structures. The answer is uncompromisingly moral, and consequently threatens to change the very terms of the question – since it subordinates political and social to moral considerations. But the threat remains only a threat, given that Zeno's discussion was set within a framework of commitment to the distinctively political ideal of concord. In Arius Didymus the threatened category shift has become a reality. The theme of the good and the bad man has now turned into an unequivocally ethical topic. Political concerns and predicates of primarily political significance certainly figure prominently in Arius Didymus' discussion, as we have seen, in line with Zeno's original preoccupations in the *Republic*. In fact the whole introductory part of S3 is devoted to material of obviously political character, as though emphasizing the political focus of the topic of the good and the bad man. The fundamental object of the exercise, however, is *simply* to demonstrate that proper application of the predicates in question is contingent on either moral goodness or moral badness, as the case may be, and to show the high moral demands imposed on political and judicial behaviour by a proper understanding of law. In consequence many of Arius Didymus's pages read oddly, as chapters of political philosophy bereft of virtually all interest in specifically political analysis – or, as one might say, depoliticized.

III

To be sure, the idea of the community of sages itself is not lost sight of. As Chapter 2 showed, it is given a prominent position at the beginning of the 'political' introductory section of S3 (II 93.19ff.). There are two points on which Stobaeus concentrates: the thesis that all goods are shared by or common to the morally good, and the notion of the concord they have with each other (which is explained in terms of the thesis about goods). Concord, of course, was the key idea of Zeno's *Republic*; and it is tempting to infer that the idea of the community of property was likewise put forward in the *Republic*. But presumably the focus on these two connected theses in Stobaeus is a reflection not of the *Republic* directly but of Chrysippus' interpretation of it.

It looks as though that interpretation may already have presented a moralized or spiritualized version of what Zeno meant if he endorsed the Pythagorean saying: κοινὰ τὰ τῶν φίλων ('What belongs to friends they hold in common'). Probably Zeno had in mind the common ownership of property, as well as the holding of women and children in common. But in the Arius Didymus passage the reference is to common 'goods', interpreted strictly in accordance with the account of *good* orthodox in Stoicism, i.e. in terms of virtue and acts of virtue. Consequently the doctrine of the community of goods is explained in terms of the benefit (ὠφέλεια) one person does to another by performing a virtuous act.

A beneficial action is counted as a *common* good because it benefits not only the person affected by it but the person who performs it.

The introductory section of S3 actually offers not one but two different and clearly rival versions of this explanation. The point of dispute seems to arise from putting the question: can a sage have goods in common with *any* other sage, or only with one known to him or living in the same place as himself? What one might call the restricted position (R) is put first, as though it were the official position (II 93.19–94.1):

> They say that all goods are common to the morally good, inasmuch as someone who benefits *his neighbour* also benefits himself.

After discussion of justice (II 94.7) and the conduct of the wise man in existing circumstances (II 94.8–20) Arius Didymus includes an account of friendship (II 94.21–95.2). Friendship too is thought of here as involving a relationship with one's neighbours. It seems likely that this restriction on the scope of friendship is due to the fact that Arius is considering friendship *as it subsists in the community of sages conceived as a community of neighbours.* Accordingly when presentation of the unrestricted or general position on common goods (G) follows next, it has the ring of a footnote to a discussion in which the notion of being neighbours has been an important feature (II 95.3–8):

> They say that goods are common in another way. For they think that everyone who benefits *anyone whatsoever* receives equal benefit due to this very thing, and that no morally bad person either is benefited or benefits. For benefiting is sustaining in accordance with virtue and being benefited is undergoing a process in accordance with virtue.

What remains unclear is the rationale of the divergence between (R) and (G).

If I am right to guess that Zeno talked of having things in common in his ideal Spartan republic, then because his republic was a city of neighbours it would be natural to interpret the things held in common in it as common to *neighbours*. So the reference to neighbours in (R) suggests an attempt to reproduce this feature of Zeno's proposals. (R) will therefore have been not only the official account but the more ancient of the two versions which appear in the introduction to S3.

(G), on the other hand, reads as though it is provoked by an objection to (R). It might be argued with respect to (R) that there is an arbitrariness in its story of what it is for there to be goods in common. According to (R) the reason why sages have goods in common is that any act whereby a sage benefits his neighbour benefits himself as well. The objection to this formulation is obvious: why does the beneficial act have to be done to a *neighbour*? If my writing this book benefits a student I know nothing about who lives in Japan, would it not follow from the principle of reflexivity incorporated in (R) that there is a good common to him or her and to me? To answer 'Yes' to this question, as it seems we must, is to accept that (G) is a more rational version of the common goods thesis than (R).

Can we discern any reason why Arius Didymus should have added (G) as a corrective footnote to (R)? It would be pleasing to think he does so because in the main part of S3 we are to be offered yet another version of the common goods thesis which is consistent with (G) but not with (R) (II 101.21–102.3):

> *All* goods are common to the morally good, and evils to the morally bad. For this reason one who benefits someone is also benefited himself, and one who harms also harms himself. *All* the morally good benefit each other, even if they are neither friends of each other at all nor kindly to one another nor approved of nor accepting (due to neither being known nor living in the same place). However they are disposed towards each other in a kindly way, and one that is friendly and approving and accepting. But the foolish are in the opposite conditions to these.

I call the doctrine of this text (U), since it implies not only (what (G) maintains) that if anyone benefits anyone the two of them have a good in common, but advances the *universal* proposition that *all* goods are common to *all* sages. (U) is presumably a better account than (R) of what we are supposing Zeno to have said in the *Republic* inasmuch as it gives a more persuasive reading of 'common'. Although (U)'s affinities are with (G) rather than with (R), it takes pains to avoid inconsistency with the notion of friendship associated with (R). For it accepts that only neighbours or those otherwise known to each other can properly speaking be friends. The cash value of the idea it substitutes for 'friend of' – i.e. 'being disposed in a friendly way towards' – is not clear. The fact that it recognizes that only a substitute notion is applicable is the interesting point.

These subtleties about friendship and kindness substitutes perhaps betray the hand of a late-ish scholastic Stoic, but the basic thesis of (U) – that all goods are common to all sages – is almost certainly Chrysippean. The consequence of holding (U) must be that any beneficial act benefits all who are in a position ever to benefit from anything, i.e. all who are wise or morally good. This doctrine is represented by Plutarch as a standard Stoic position (*Comm. not.* 1068 F):

> If a single sage anywhere at all extends his finger prudently, all the sages throughout the inhabited world are benefited. This is the job they assign to friendship; this is how, by the beneficial acts common to the sages, the virtues are brought to fulfilment.

He goes on to talk in terms which echo the absence of restrictions as to knowledge and neighbouring referred to in Arius Didymus' presentation of (U) (1069 A):

> the amazing benefit which sages receive from the virtuous motions of one another even if they are not together and happen not even to be acquainted.

A little later he attributes to Chrysippus a specific consequence of the position (1076 A):

> Zeus and Dion, being wise, are benefited alike by each other whenever the one encounters a movement of the other. For this, not anything else, is the good that men get of gods and gods of men, once they have become sages.

(R) and (G) are not exactly commonsensical ideas, but of course the notion of the reflexivity of benefit and harm is thoroughly Socratic, and easy enough to accept if one agrees with e.g. Plato and Aristotle that the exercise of virtue is a good enhancing the happiness of the agent. (U), by contrast, is highly counter-intuitive. It is presumably significant that whereas (R) and (G) are derived *from* the premiss (B) that if someone benefits another he also benefits himself, (U) is not itself argued, but is presented rather as the basis of an inference *to* (B). If every beneficial act benefits *all* sages, then it will obviously follow that whenever a sage performs a beneficial act he will benefit himself – given that he is one sage among the rest. The sort of justification Chrysippus would doubtless have wished to give for (U) itself would likewise involve looking at things from the point of view of the whole, not of ourselves the parts. Thus the physical story envisaged would presumably consist in explaining that any act of virtue enhances the tension of the *pneuma* which is the vehicle of the *logos* that controls and pervades the universe, and so benefits all those whose portion of that *logos* is in a condition capable of being benefited, as a sage's *logos* is.

S3, then, contains two main statements of the proposition that goods are common to those who are morally good. (R), in the introductory section, appears to represent a moralizing Chrysippean interpretation of what may originally have been a doctrine of Zeno's *Republic*. It holds merely that any act benefiting one's neighbour constitutes a good common to the neighbour benefited and the person who benefits him or her. It is an idea which can readily be defended on ethical grounds within the framework of any ancient system which makes virtuous acts functions or constituents of happiness. (U), in the main section, is a much more ambitious thesis, once more probably the work of Chrysippus, and perhaps another shot by him at explaining what Zeno was driving at in the *Republic*. It makes *all* goods, including all beneficial acts, common to *all* sages, whether they know each other or live in the same place or not. It can be defended only with resources drawn from metaphysical monism; and understanding it requires us to adopt the point of view of the whole.

IV

The questions which Stoicism addressed in devising (G) and (U) are plausibly regarded (as with (R)) as at least partly exegetical questions. But why did they arise in the first place? Why, for example, should the concept of *neighbour* have become the focus of scrutiny? They would certainly be adequately explained by a desire to reflect upon Zeno's *Republic* in the light of the doctrine of the cosmic city, and to adapt Zeno's conception of a community of sages to the notion of the community of rational beings who are citizens of the universe. That this was in fact the root motivation is suggested by the evidence of the contents of Book III of Chrysippus' *On Nature* (reviewed in Chapter 3). For we know that in a book which presented the doctrine of the cosmic city Chrysippus also argued that the morally good exercise the same virtue as Zeus, in terms very similar to those in which he talked of the good common to Zeus and Dion and more generally to gods and men. It is a natural inference that this treatment of the goods common to men and gods also appeared in *On Nature* III, and that it belonged to his discussion of the cosmic city.

If so, the verdict of Section I needs revision. It is not that later Stoic tradition *ignored* Zeno's republic of sages in favour of the cosmic city. It is rather that in advancing the theory of the cosmic city Chrysippus had already assimilated the core doctrines of the *Republic* – the city of sages and the thesis that they hold things in common – to central elements in the theory. It was not rational to restrict community of goods to neighbours, nor membership of the city to humans only, when all rational beings, gods and men (at least when they have attained moral goodness), are indistinguishable in virtue. Probably Chrysippus did not see himself as correcting Zeno here, but simply as drawing out more clearly the logical consequences of Zeno's own ideas.

From the vantage point of history the *Republic* accordingly has the look of a fascinatingly 'Janus-facing' piece of theory. If Chapter 2 of this book is correct, Zeno wrote it as a contribution to the dialectic of classical Greek philosophy about the proper constitution of the *polis*. His solution was briefer and simpler than any previous thinker had worked out, without therefore ceasing to engage with the problems of how a group of persons known to one another and living together may achieve the concord necessary for survival and happiness. As a piece of classical political theory, however, the *Republic* contained the seeds of its own destruction. Or to put the point more positively, it opened the way for doing political philosophy in a quite different style, no longer tied to preoccupation with the *polis*, but focused instead on the moral potentialities of man considered as man, not as citizen.

The idea of the cosmic city can be seen in this light as a concept which mediates the transition from republicanism to natural law theory. For the doctrine of the cosmic city attempts to retain community and citizenship while removing all contingency – such as physical proximity or mutual acquaintance – from the notion of citizenship. What citizenship now consists in is nothing but obedience by a plurality of persons to the injunctions of right reason on the just treatment of other persons: i.e. to law as nature formulates it. Such a conception of the citizen is manifestly unstable. The thesis that social morality flows from adherence to the dictates of natural law so understood does not *require* for its intelligibility or acceptability any reference to citizenship at all. It is a thesis solely about what is enjoined upon man or any rational social animal *qua* rational social animal. Consequently we should not be surprised to find the idea of natural law put to work in social ethics in contexts which make no appeal to the divine city or to a metaphysical theory of providence. In short, the stage is set for *ius naturale* as it appears in Cicero's *de officiis* and the *Digest* – and in Grotius, Pufendorf and beyond.[1]

[1] This chapter seemed not to need annotation. But it may be of interest to acknowledge that the idea for its theme was suggested by reading J.G.A. Pocock, 'Virtues, rights and manners: A model for historians of political thought', in his collection *Virtue, Commerce, and History* (Cambridge 1985) 37–50 – although of course its ultimate origins are Hegelian: cf. e.g. C. Taylor, *Hegel* (Cambridge 1975), p. 385.

Appendix A

Zeno and Alexander

Plutarch, *de Alex. virt.* 329 A–B translates as follows:

> The much admired *Republic* of Zeno, who founded the Stoic sect, is aimed at this one main point, that our arrangement for habitations should not be based on cities or peoples,[1] each one distinguished by its own special system of justice, but we should regard all men as citizens and members of the populace, and there should be one way of life and one order, like that of a herd grazing together and nurtured by a common law/pasturing (νόμος). This Zeno wrote, picturing as it were a dream or image of a philosopher's well-regulated republic, but it was Alexander who gave effect to the theory.

According to the argument of Chapter I Zeno's city is conceived as an ideal Spartan republic. Plutarch takes it to be a blueprint for the world-wide community which on his account Alexander tried to promote. The general spirit of the two conceptions is quite different.

Scholars have sometimes gone further and alleged actual incompatibilities between Plutarch's account and our other evidence about the *Republic*. Most of these allegations are inconclusive, as e.g. Baldry and

[1] 'Peoples' translates δήμους (cf. 'members of the populace' for δημότας below). Scholars sometimes render 'demes' or 'parishes' (so e.g. A.A. Long and D.N. Sedley, *The Hellenistic Philosophers* I (Cambridge 1987), p. 429, from whose translation I have elsewhere borrowed), no doubt in order to achieve a contrast with 'cities', πόλεις. But as Baldry noted (*JHS* 79 (1959) 13 n. 19) Plutarch a little later describes Alexander's project as designed to make all men one people (δῆμον) (330 D); and if the argument of this Appendix is correct, one might well expect reminiscences of later Stoic ideas and terminology in the passage: Clement, *Strom.* IV 26 p. 642 P [= *SVF* III 327] couples the words ἡ πόλις καὶ ὁ δῆμος (in a syntactically obscure sentence), as though they were effectively synonymous.

Erskine have shown.[2] But two singled out by Baldry deserve further examination. First, according to Plutarch we are to regard all men as our fellow-citizens, whereas D.L. VII 32–3 made only the good or wise citizens. On further inspection this difficulty dissolves. For in developing his account of Alexander's project Plutarch continues (329 C):

> He instructed all to think of the whole inhabited world as their fatherland, his camp as their acropolis and garrison, the morally good as their kin, the morally bad as foreigners.

The meaning of 'all' is notoriously context-dependent. Plutarch's loose and expansive mode of expression is one he is prepared to invest with more Stoic precision, as here, as suits his rhetorical purposes: 'all' now effectively becomes 'all the good'. A second inconsistency is not so easily explained away. Plutarch's claim that for Zeno our way of life should *not* be based on cities appears to be incompatible with his concern for 'the safety of the city' (Athen. 561 C) and his provision that in cities (note the plural) there should be no temples, law courts or gymnasia (D.L. VII 33). It is true (as Baldry and Erskine both stress) that Plutarch puts the emphasis not on the inappropriateness of cities as such, but on the wrongness of there being separate systems of justice in different cities rather than a single common law. But this does not alter the fact that the other evidence seems to envisage cities which *are* the focus of their citizens' moral and political concern. Baldry and Erskine try to remove the difficulty along similar lines. They suppose that the Plutarch passage is envisaging the one true ideal unified society. It consists of a plurality of local communities (*poleis*) which are the subject of the Athenaeus text on concord and security and of Cassius the Sceptic's report about temples etc.. But because these *poleis* are deprived of so many of the functions and characteristics of the traditional Greek *polis* the Plutarch text can fairly represent Zeno as abolishing the organization of living arrangements on the basis of *poleis*. This solution is unpersuasive: it leaves the word *polis*, taken as bearing one and the same reference, both having (Athenaeus) and not having (Plutarch) strong positive resonance; and it makes both the *polis* and the ideal unified society the focus of Zeno's concern for harmony. The fact is that nobody who read just the Plutarch passage or, on the other hand, just the Athenaeus and Diogenes Laertius texts, would ever dream that Zeno's views were so complicated.

[2] Baldry, *JHS* 79 (1959) 12–13; Erskine, *The Hellenistic Stoa*. pp. 18–22.

Perhaps better attempts to reconcile Plutarch with the other evidence in this area could be devised, or resort made to some developmental hypothesis about Zeno's thought.[3] There is not much point in attempting the task, however, before one has addressed the prior question: is there reason to judge Plutarch's information *reliable*? It is not hard to find grounds for a negative answer.

For one thing, all the other texts considered in Chapters 1 and 2 are doxographical in kind. They evidently derive from sources which aimed to report individual bits of doctrine, whether or not they had axes to grind as well. While the selection of material may be biased and comments on it partisan, there is not much sign of tendentiousness in the reports themselves. And they cohere very well with other accounts of early Stoic doctrine. By contrast, Plutarch's essay and its sequel on the same subject are rhetorical exercises, 'devoid of any serious purpose'.[4] The passage which concerns us claims to provide a broad view of the 'main point' of the *Republic*, not specific details of its contents. It is obviously essential to the author's argument that Alexander's exploits and ambitions and Zeno's philosophical ideas should be presented as convergent. Accordingly there is no particular reason to expect him to set much store by accuracy and precision here on points of philosophy. Certainly the treatment of Alexander is consistently exaggerated. Incidents in his career which receive restrained treatment in Plutarch's *Life* are frequently given grandiose interpretations in the essays. For example, 'his reply to those who urged him to compete in the Olympic Games [ch. 9] is supposed to prove him a philosopher, while in the *Life* (ch. 4) it is properly used to

[3] This was the expedient to which W.W. Tarn had resort in his *Alexander the Great* (Cambridge 1948), vol. II, pp. 417–23. It founders principally upon the difficulty that Plutarch refers to the ideas he attributes to Zeno as the focus of his πολιτεία: Tarn has to argue that πολιτεία here means merely 'constitution', not the book-title *Republic*, but this is a desperate manoeuvre. Nonetheless Tarn discerned a real inconcinnity between this Plutarch passage and the other evidence on the *Republic* which subsequent scholars have not taken seriously enough.

[4] I borrow this verdict from J.R. Hamilton, *Plutarch: Alexander*. A Commentary (Oxford 1969), p. xxxi, who rightly calls it 'the obvious view'. Section II of his Introduction (pp. xxiii–xxxiii) provides a good recent guide to the two speeches *de Alexandri Magni fortuna et virtute* and to scholarly discussion of them. The verdict is broadly shared by D. Babut, *Plutarque et le Stoïcisme* (Paris 1969), pp. 84–5, who judges that Plutarch employs Stoic themes in a superficial way 'à des fins purement rhétoriques et formelles'. For the criticisms of Alexander to which Plutarch was presumably responding see G. Giannantoni, 'Cinici e stoici su Alessandro Magno', in G. Casertano (ed.), *I filosofi e il potere nella società e nella cultura antiche* (Naples 1989); cf. also P.A. Brunt, 'From Epictetus to Arrian', *Athenaeum* 55 (1977) 19–48.

show that he did not desire every kind of *doxa*'.[5] Few today, and probably not even Plutarch when he wrote, believe that Alexander was any sort of philosopher[6] or that his campaigns were conceived in the hope of instituting a single community of all good men everywhere. It would be odd to place implicit trust in every word of what is said about Zeno's views when we give no credence at all to what we are told about Alexander's.

Nor does the detail of the Plutarch text inspire much confidence in its reliability. The most questionable feature is the comparison of the universal society Zeno is supposed to advocate with a herd grazing together and nurtured by a common law. The image of the people as herd and of the king as herdsman is a popular one in Greek literature and philosophy from Homer on (cf. *Il.* II 243 etc.).[7] Although it recurs, e.g. in Dio Chrysostom (e.g. I 13, III 41, IV 44–5) and in pseudo-Pythagorean political writings (Stob. IV 5.61, 7.64 = pp. 36.4–5, 82.5–6 Thesleff), it is not put by them to major theoretical use. The *loci classici* in texts of political theory are the first page of Xenophon's *Cyropaedia* (I 1.2) and Plato's *Politicus* 265–8, 274–6, where the conception of king as herdsman is subjected to critical scrutiny and effectively abandoned, to be revived in the pseudo-Platonic *Minos*. All the vocabulary Plutarch uses in making the analogy is found (with related terms) in Plato, in particularly heavy concentration at *Politicus* 267–8 (ἀγέλη, *Polit.* 265–8 *passim*; σύννομος, *Leg.* 666 E [cf. συννομή, *Polit.* 268 C]; συντρέφομαι, *Leg.* 752 C [cf. τροφή, *Polit.* 276 D, etc.; τροφός, 268 A, C]). The play on νόμος as (1) law (2) pasturing is prefigured in the *Minos* 317 D-318 A. So far as I can find, this cluster of imagery does not reflect a Stoic view of kingship or statesmanship. Users of von Arnim might be tempted to think otherwise by *SVF* III 332. This reproduces a passage of Clement (*Strom.* I 169 p. 421 P) where legislation is defended as a science which oversees and cares for the herd of men. Clement's vocabulary here obviously exploits the jargon of Greek philosophy, but it must be borne in mind that he is also exploiting the scriptural text (*Ev. Joh.* X 11): 'The good shepherd lays down his life for his sheep.' There is no clear echo of Stoicism at this point (as there is elsewhere in the context), and no obvious way of telling how far he is reproducing an earlier philosophical definition and how far he is using the resources of Greek philosophy to make his own definition. Needless to say

[5] So Hamilton, *Plutarch: Alexander*, p. xxxii.

[6] Its status as Plutarchean fiction is supported by the fact that at *Lycurgus* 31 Lycurgus is made to play just the same sort of role vis-à-vis Plato, Zeno and Diogenes as Alexander does vis-à-vis Zeno here.

[7] For a good brief discussion of this topic see J.B. Skemp, *Plato's Statesman* (London 1952), pp. 52–66.

the early Christians were fond of describing both mankind in general and the church in particular as a herd or flock (ἀγέλη: see Lampe, *Patristic Greek Lexicon* (Oxford 1961) s.v.). It is not only in texts which might be classified as political theory that this vocabulary is used. It is also found in anthropological or zoological contexts. Aristotle divides animals into the solitary (μοναδικά) and the gregarious (ἀγελαῖα) (*HA* I 1, 487 b34); man clearly falls in the second category (*Pol.* I 2, 1253 a1–9; *EN* I 7, 1097 a8–11). The most striking later development of these Aristotelian thoughts known to me is in Philo Judaeus. Philo knows the division between gregarious and solitary as a purely zoological classification (III 48.10 Cohn-Wendland). But in *Cherub.* 58 (I 184. 14–17 CW) he refers to Adam and Eve as 'a long way from being gregarious animals which graze together (τῶν συννόμων καὶ ἀγελαίων), but like solitary animals, following solitary ways'. And a fragment of the questions on *Genesis* (no. 11 of the Greek fragments as presented in the Loeb edition (*Philo* Supplementary Vol. II (1961)) of R. Marcus) makes the thoroughly Aristotelian claim (a little Stoicized at the end):

> Nature has made man not like the solitary beasts but highly social like the gregarious animals which graze together (ὡς ἀγελαῖα καὶ σύννομα κοινικώτατον): so that he might live not for himself alone, but for his father and mother and brothers and wife and children and his other relations and his friends and his fellow-citizens and his tribesmen and his country and those of the same race and all men.

All things considered, there is not much reason to suppose the herd comparison in our Plutarch passage is authentically Zenonian. Plutarch is drawing on the *lingua franca* of Greek thought, probably the more unhesitatingly because of the Platonic associations of the idea, in order to embellish his presentation of Zeno's doctrine.[8]

It might be suggested that this conclusion can be accepted without

[8] I do not assert that Stoics later than Zeno never use a herd or flock analogy in political contexts. For one example, see Hierocles' description of man as ζῶον συναγελαστικόν (col. XI 14 von Arnim), which supports an explanation of why men *do* live in cities; also Antipater, *ap.* Stob. IV 507. 11–13, where however there is nothing in either thought or vocabulary reminiscent of our Plutarch passage. It is interesting that when Plutarch elsewhere alludes to the Stoic doctrine of the cosmic city (*Comm. not.* 1065 F), (1) he once more employs the vocabulary of συννομή: 'a town (ἄστυ) common to gods and men who are to graze together (συννομησομένων) in justice and virtue concordantly (ὁμολογουμένως) and blissfully', but (2) never elsewhere in the numerous references to the cosmic city in other authors does this vocabulary recur (ἄστυ is also idiosyncratic). This is clear confirmation that it is Plutarchean, not Stoic.

impugning the Zenonian credentials of the passage as a whole: Plutarch could himself have supplied the analogy to support otherwise genuinely Zenonian material. But there are other elements in the wording of the text which arouse suspicion. 'One way of life (βίος)', says Plutarch, 'and one order (κόσμος).' (1) Once again I am unable to find in texts representing the views of the early Stoics any subsequent use of κόσμος in the sense of an ordering of society. The expression seems to be used exclusively of the physical universe, even if the universe so designated is sometimes viewed *as* a cosmic city or society.[9] On the other hand κόσμος is certainly employed by Plutarch himself in just the same way, to mean 'social order' a little later in his essay (329 F). He says of Alexander's decision to prefer Persian to Median dress on grounds of thrift that he took it 'looking to this order'. This appears to be a reference back to 329 C–D where Plutarch continues the passage quoted above (p. 105) as follows:

> [He instructed them] to distinguish Greek and barbarian not by cloak or light shield [i.e. typical Greek costume/arms] nor by scimitar or jacket [i.e. typically barbarian arms/garb], but to take virtue as the sign of Greekness, vice that of the barbarous; and to regard clothes, food, marriages, habits of life (διαίτας) as common to all, blended together by blood-ties and children.[10]

Simplicity of dress, not any kind of elaborateness, is more consonant with virtue and the obliteration of cultural differences. (2) As with κόσμος, so with βίος. The relatively few texts which deal with the teaching of the early Stoics on the relations of the wise with each other do not claim that they lead a single way of life, as Zeno is represented as urging us to do in the present passage. But Plutarch makes Alexander 'mix up ways of life (βίους), characters, marriages, habits as in a loving cup, so bringing together into the same [system] practices from everywhere'. It is impossible to work out whether 'one way of life and one order' really reflects anything Zeno actually said in the *Republic*. The balance of probability is that Plutarch, having decided to attribute the idea to Alexander, has then *himself* written it (at least as so expressed) *into* Zeno's script.

Presumably, however, Plutarch would not have fathered either this

[9] Zeno seems to have used the verb κοσμεῖν to mean 'adorn': Clem. *Paidag.* III 11,74 p. 296 P, of perfumes, gold jewellery and the like; Stob. *Flor.* 43,88 Mein.: 'Zeno said that cities should be adorned not with votive offerings but with the virtues of their inhabitants' (very likely a reference to the *Republic*).

[10] Babut, *Plutarque et le Stoïcisme*, pp. 356–9, shows the obsessiveness of Plutarch's pan-Hellenist preoccupation with the distinction between Greek and barbarian, evidenced in both *Lives* and *Moralia*.

notion or the herd analogy upon the *Republic* unless there was already something in the work which invited this treatment. The one incontrovertibly Stoic idea and expression not just in the latter part of the text but in the entire passage is νόμος κοινός: common law. The concept of a divine natural law prescribing right and forbidding wrong is ascribed elsewhere to Zeno.[11] It figures prominently, now designated κοινὸς νόμος, in Cleanthes' *Hymn to Zeus*.[12] There is no doubt that it was taken up by Chrysippus as a fundamental Stoic doctrine, of crucial importance to much physical and ethical theory, including the theory of the cosmic city, where, as the 'right reason which pervades all things' (D.L. VII 88), it is conceived as a moral principle common to gods and men alike.[13] It seems likely enough that (1) it was a key principle of Zeno's *Republic*, such that Plutarch could reasonably have referred to it as 'the one main point' of the work, and (2) its presence in the *Republic* inspired both Plutarch's introduction of the herd analogy and his assimilation of Zeno's ideas (probably under the influence of the later idea of the cosmic city) to what he took to be Alexander's programme of cultural homogenization.[14]

What use did the *Republic* itself make of the principle? Plutarch's suggestion that it was employed to advocate a universal society must be regarded as highly suspect.[15] It is difficult to reconcile with the other evidence about the *Republic*. And Plutarch's methods and rhetorical purposes in *de Alex. virt.* generate no conviction about his dependability in this matter. I conjecture that Zeno was actually making a quite different point: that the source of moral authority in any city of the good and wise is not man-made justice or variable convention, but the common law of nature.[16] Appeal to the common law would have given him exactly the

[11] Cic. *ND* I 36; Lact. *Inst.* I 5; Minuc. Fel. *Octav.* 19, 10 [=*SVF* I 162].

[12] Stob. I 26.13, 27.4 (lines 24,39). Cleanthes' poem points, of course, to the ultimate source of the idea in Heraclitus (esp. Fr. 114).

[13] So e.g. Cic. *Leg.* I 23, M. Aurelius IV 4 (but without the reference to gods). For further discussion see Chapter 3 above.

[14] There is no reason to doubt that Plutarch *did* have some real knowledge of the *Republic* when he wrote *de Alex. virt.*. The passage cited above on common clothes, food, marriages, etc. and on blending 'by blood-ties and children' is close enough to what we learn of the *Republic* at D.L. VII 33 to make scepticism on this point unreasonable.

[15] Plutarch is perhaps running Zeno's employment of the concept together with the sort of thinking reflected in Cicero *Rep.* III 33, with its denial of the appropriateness of separate systems of law and justice in different states.

[16] An early and doubtless influential instance of this style of thinking about law, which may indeed have done something to shape Zeno's views, is of course Plato *Leg.* 713 E–715 D. But its ultimate source, acknowledged by the Stoics, was Heraclitus, especially Fr. 114 DK (cf. n. 12 above).

appropriate weapon for defending the antinomian measures which are listed in D.L. VII 32–3: the κοινὸς νόμος is the only law which should command our obedience. The conjecture receives support from the fact that the standard Stoic definition of a city explains it as 'a plurality of men administered by law' (Clem. *Strom.* IV 26 p. 642 P), for here the notion of law – presumably natural or divine law – is again central to their thinking about the city.[17]

[17] Cf. also Chrysippus' book-title *On City and Law* (Phld. *On the Stoics*, col. XV. 26–7).

Appendix B

Problems with the Stoic definitions of love

Definition [A] (see Chapter 2, p. 29) has the effect of restricting love to the wise or at least the morally serious: at any rate, the object of love is specified as possessing a property (natural endowment for virtue) which not everyone who might be called a lover could be expected to respond to. There is reason to think that the author of [B] took deliberate pains to make his definition more truly general in application. In Stob. II 66.9–11 [B] is preceded by the observation:

> Loving itself is only an indifferent, since it sometimes happens to the morally bad also.

There seems to be a contrast with loving nobly (καλῶς, II 66.8), which is what the science of love is concerned with (II 66.3–9). Love can be prompted in anybody by the beauty of young people who are 'blooming': it is the sage in virtue of his understanding or science of love who will love in noble fashion those naturally endowed for virtue. The point comes over nicely at Stob. II 115.1–4:

> Love is an attempt to make friends, on account of beauty being apparent, with young people in bloom. Which is why the sage will also be expert in love (ἐρωτικόν), and will love those worthy of love, i.e. those well-born and naturally endowed.

Since Stob. II 66.3–11 seems to echo [A] when it specifies his science or expertise as 'knowledge of the chase after naturally endowed young people', it is tempting to conjecture that the author of [B] was deliberately correcting [A] in distinguishing love itself and the love of the sage.

But [B] in its turn has difficulties. I discuss two of them:

(1) That love is a response to physical beauty is indicated by Zeno when he speaks of those who *manifest by their appearance* (ἐμφαινόμενον διὰ τοῦ εἴδους) endowment for virtue. This formulation presumably explains [B]'s choice of the word ἐμφαινόμενον (in some versions ἔμφασις). But

where Zeno made beauty the *vehicle* of ἔμφασις, i.e. of the manifestation of endowment for virtue, in [B] beauty is itself the thing that is said to be ἐμφαινόμενον. And this shift seems to carry with it a change in sense or force from 'manifest' to '(merely) apparent', since otherwise [B] could have said simply 'on account of beauty'. So [B]'s use of ἐμφαινόμενον / ἔμφασις turns out to be no more than a verbal echo of Zeno's wording; and 'beauty being apparent' / 'an appearance of beauty' is in fact an interpretation of Zeno's τοῦ εἴδους, 'appearance'.

As may be inferred from Plutarch *Comm. not.* ch. 28, 1072 F ff., the interpretation is part of an attempt to think out a basically Zenonian view of love in the light of the Stoic paradox: 'only the wise man is beautiful'. Since the love of the wise is focused on persons who are not *yet* virtuous, and so not yet sages,[1] it follows if we assume the truth of the paradox that no beautiful person is a proper object of love, and that the young man or woman who is, is ugly. It must therefore be the mere appearance of beauty which prompts love. Would Zeno have welcomed this interpretation? Perhaps he would have wished to avoid calling the youthful objects of the sage's love 'beautiful'. But I doubt that the equation of their physical attractiveness with a mere appearance of beauty would have satisfied him either.

(2) The author of [B] might object to the account of his position given in the previous two paragraphs. He could point out that it pays no attention to his inclusion of the words 'with young people in bloom' (νεῶν ὡραίων). For perhaps this addition is meant to capture the real physical attractiveness of the typical object of love, without implying that it is real beauty (i.e. real moral or spiritual beauty), and without *equating* it with the characteristic manifestation which is the particular *sort* of bloom that attracts not all, but noble love.

I hope that this is what [B] envisages. But if so, [B] was certainly misunderstood in the Stoa itself. For at the end of the section on love, D.L. VII 130 records the following explanation:

> And they say that the bloom (τὴν ὥραν) is the flower of virtue.

[1] Sextus (*M* XI 170) offers the following syllogism as Stoic:

> The person worthy of love is beautiful.
> Only the sage is worthy of love.
> So only the sage is beautiful.

He is bluffing. Zeno clearly did not hold the second premiss, nor did Stoic orthodoxy depart from his view (Stob. II 115.3–4). And [B], the standard definition, speaks only of apparent beauty: the first premiss is only dubiously Stoic.

This is evidently an attempt to make sense of 'young people in bloom' in the full version of [B]. The attempt obviously does not work. On Zeno's story, the youthful object of the sage's love is not yet virtuous – not yet in full flower – but merely naturally endowed for virtue. Moreover, if I am right [B] aims at an account of love which is ethically neutral in any case.

Perhaps this kind of difficulty about the meaning of 'bloom' is one reason for the omission of the words 'with young people in bloom' in nearly all examples of [B] in the sources. Sextus may or may not be rubbing salt in the wound when (to illustrate a logical term) he says (*M* VII 239):

> The person who says that love is 'an attempt to make friends' coindicates (συνεμφαίνει, lit. simultaneously makes apparent) 'with young persons in bloom', even if he does not expressly bring this out. For nobody loves old persons or people who do not have the bloom of the prime of love.

Appendix C

Ethical attractivness

There is a fascinating extract from Zeno preserved in Clement which is one of our best pieces of evidence for Stoic physiognomics (Clem. *Paidagogos* III 11, 74 pp. 296–7 P = *SVF* I 246). The text is a bit tricky, so I present the version I propose to read.

> καλὴν τινα καὶ ἀξιέραστον[1] ὑπογράφειν ὁ Κιτιεὺς ἔοικε Ζήνων εἰκόνα νεανίου[2] καὶ οὕτως αὐτὸν ἀνδριαντουργεῖ· ἔστω, φησί, καθαρὸν τὸ πρόσωπον, ὀφρὺς μὴ καθειμένη μηδὲ ὄμμα ἀναπεπταμένον μηδὲ ἀνακεκλασμένον,[3] μὴ ὕπτιος ὁ τράχηλος μηδὲ ἀνιέμενα τὰ τοῦ σώματος μέλη, ἀλλὰ [τὰ][4] μετέωρα ἐντόνοις ὅμοια, ὀρθὸν οὖς[5] πρὸς τὸν λόγον [ὀξύτης καὶ κατοκωχὴ τῶν ὀρθῶς εἰρημένων][6] καὶ σχηματισμοὶ καὶ κίνησις μηδὲν

[1] These first four words are treated as belonging with the previous sentence by editors (see e.g. W. Dindorf, *Clementis Alexandrini Opera* (Oxford 1869), I 384), rounding off the quotation from the First Epistle of Peter it finishes with: 'so that you may inherit a blessing' (ἵνα εὐλογίαν κληρονομήσητε, *Ep. Petr.* I 3.9). It makes much better sense to connect them with what follows, especially if I am right to see the passage as a description of the manifestation of natural endowment for virtue which attracts the love of the sage.

[2] The MSS have νεανίδα or νεανία. Neither works grammatically, but Dindorf (ad loc.) gives a plausible argument for taking νεανία as the scribe's idiosyncratic variant for νεανίου. A masculine noun is needed to be the referent of αὐτόν.

[3] Cobet, followed by subsequent editors, conjectured διακεκλασμένον, 'soft', 'enervated' (*Mnemosyne* 11 (1862) 387). But LSJ s.v. ἀνακλάω quotes Hp. *Coac.* as using ἀνακεκλασμένοι of the eyelids as 'slightly open'. Zeno is contrasting the pert or flirtatious wide-eyed look with the no less sexy but slier or more smouldering look from under the eyelids. It is crucial that the adjectives both refer to *physical* states of the eyes in the first instance, not to emotional properties.

[4] τὰ is persuasively excised by C. Wachsmuth, in the first instalment of his *Commentationes de Zenone Citiensi et Cleanthe Assio* (Göttingen 1874), p. 6.

[5] ὀρθὸν οὖς: Cobet's excellent conjecture for the meaningless ὀρθονου of the MSS. (*Mnemosyne* 6 (1857) 339–40), accepted by Dindorf, but rejected in favour of ὀρθὸς νοῦς by Wachsmuth (*ibid.*), whose reading is adopted in *SVF* and by A.C. Pearson, *The Fragments of Zeno and Cleanthes* (Cambridge 1891), pp. 207–8. Once again, we need a reference to something physical – to a part of the body.

[6] Dindorf (*Clementis Alexandrini Opera*) excised ὀξύτης as a gloss on ὀρθὸν οὖς.

> ἐνδιδοῦσα τοῖς ἀκολάστοις ἐλπίδος αἰδὼς μὲν ἐπανθείτω καὶ ἀρρενωπία, ἀπέστω δὲ καὶ ὁ ἀπὸ τῶν μυροπωλίων καὶ χρυσοχοείων καὶ ἐριοπωλίων ἄλυς καὶ ὁ ἀπὸ τῶν ἄλλων ἐργαστηρίων, ἔνθα ἑταιρικῶς κεκοσμημέναι[7] ὥσπερ ἐπὶ τέγους καθεζόμεναι[7] διημερεύουσιν.

> Zeno of Citium seems to sketch a beautiful and properly loveable image of a young man. He sculpts him like this:
>
> Let his countenance be pure; his brow not relaxed; his eye not wide open nor half-closed; his neck not thrown back; nor the limbs of his body relaxed, but keyed up like strings under tension; his ear cocked for the *logos*; and his bearing and movement giving no hope to the licentious. Let modesty and a manly look flower upon him, but away with the excitement of perfumers' shops and goldsmiths and wool shops – and indeed all the other shops, where women spend the whole day adorned like courtesans, as though they were sitting in a brothel.

Clement does not state that this is a verbatim quotation. But the pithy style is in Zeno's manner. And if he delivered his account as a sequence of crisp third-person imperatives, it is difficult to conceive why Clement should have bothered to rewrite it. The passage comes in Book III of the *Paidagogos*, which is devoted to discussion of true beauty. Chapter 11 is mostly on dress.

There is good reason to take Zeno's advice on physical bearing to be inspired by a conception of that physical attractiveness which he took to

This is on the right lines: but the entire phrase in square brackets should be explained in these terms. 'Acuteness and comprehension of what is said correctly' is an ancient reader's attempt to understand the whole expression 'ear cocked for the *logos*'. It misses the primary *physical* reference of Zeno's original.

7 Cobet (*Mnem.* 6 (1857) 339–40) well saw that the passage as a whole had to constitute advice to a young *man*, not a young woman, despite νεανίδα in many MSS, although apart from noting the oddness of ἀρρενωπία urged upon a woman his arguments were not good (Dindorf's observation that αὐτόν needs a masculine referent is the clinching consideration). But he then regarded himself as obliged to convert the females made up like courtesans into males. So he turns the participles into masculines. Subsequent editors follow suit. This is absurd. The point is that young men should stay away from these places, for among their other snares is the presence of women of easy virtue. And the next sentence *requires* a contrast with women: 'So then let not men either spend time in barbers' shops or retailers chatting and prattling away, and let them stop chasing the women who go by.'

'manifest natural endowment for virtue' and to be what motivates the wise person's attempt to make friends. The advice would clearly have no point unless the physical attitudes recommended were morally desirable. And at one point talk of flowering or being in bloom (ἐπανθείτω) is explicitly introduced, reminding us of the official school definition [B] of the concept of love (Stob. II 115.1–2):

> Love is an attempt to make friends, on account of beauty being apparent, with young people in bloom (νέων ὡραίων).

Clement's use of the word ἀξιέραστος, 'properly loveable', in introducing the Zeno extract, may be borrowed from whatever Stoic source he was using, for this comparatively rare expression figures in the account of expertise in love which follows the definition (Stob. II 115.2–4):

> Which is why the sage will also be expert in love (ἐρωτικόν), and will love those worthy of love (ἀξιεράστων), i.e. those well-born and naturally endowed.

This circumstance lends support to Wachsmuth's conjecture (*Commentationes* I, p. 6) that Zeno's advice was to be found in his *Art of love* (D.L. VII 34).

Zeno is urging young men to *aim for* a particular sort of physical bearing. But the wise man will love those well-born and naturally endowed. Must we not infer that the recipient of Zeno's advice is conceived of as *not* naturally endowed and so *not* worthy of love? A further passage of Arius Didymus suggests that some such puzzle as this generated a dispute in the Stoa (Stob. II 107.14–108.4):

> On the naturally endowed, and again on the well-born, some of those in the school have been carried into saying that every wise man is of this sort, but others not. For the first party think that people become naturally endowed for virtue not only from nature but also in some cases from preparation. And they approve of the proverbial saying:
>
> Practice over time turns into nature.
>
> They have taken a similar line over good birth, too, so that natural endowment is generically a state appropriate (οἰκείαν) for virtue produced by nature or by preparation, or a state in virtue of which there are people with a good capacity for acquiring virtue, and good birth is a state appropriate for virtue produced by family or by preparation.

The Stoics who get the lion's share of Arius Didymus' exposition would have no difficulty with the proposition that a young man acting on Zeno's advice in the Clement text may become naturally endowed and so a proper object of love.

Appendix D

Descending to marriage

Diogenes Laertius reports (VII 121):

> They say that the wise man will take part in politics if nothing prevents it, as Chrysippus says in the first book of *On Lives*. For he will restrain vice and encourage virtue. He will marry, as Zeno says in the *Republic*, and have children.

What is ascribed to Zeno here is on the face of it in flat contradiction with the testimony elsewhere in Diogenes (VII 131) that the *Republic* advocated that women should be held in common and that sexual relations between men and women should be promiscuous. This initial impression is reinforced by the report in the doxographical section of the life of Diogenes the Cynic (VI 72), very similar in wording to VII 131:

> He used to say that women should be held in common, recognizing no convention of marriage (γάμον μηδένα νομίζων), but holding that a man and a woman should have sexual relations provided only that each persuades the other.

The difficulty about the Zenonian evidence has been much discussed.[1] The main solutions favoured have been: (1) D.L. VII 121 reflects later Stoic doctrine – the reference to Zeno's *Republic* is a mistake; (2) it *does* accurately report the *Republic*, specifying the conduct appropriate to the wise man in ordinary circumstances, not what he should do in a community of the good and wise; (3) not only does it faithfully report the *Republic* but it can readily be related to the common regime for women, provided we take the word γαμήσειν (translated 'marry') as meaning not much more than 'mate'. None of these suggestions is *prima facie* very attractive: (1) because it seems facile and arbitrary; (2) because there is no other evi-

[1] For an excellent brief account see Baldry, *JHS* 79 (1959) 9–10.

dence of concern in the *Republic* with how the sage should behave in ordinary circumstances; (3) because the comparison with VI 72 shows it to be highly unlikely that Diogenes Laertius, at any rate, intended γαμήσειν to carry such weak implications.

Our first task must be to try and establish the doxographical context to which the remark about marriage at D.L. VII 121 belongs. There is no great difficulty in this, thanks to the availability of plenty of comparative material. We begin with the doxographical schemes summarized by Arius Didymus before his own presentations of Stoic and Peripatetic ethics.[2]

In Philo of Larisa's scheme there is a section on lives (βίοι), i.e. ways of life, subdivided into a 'special' and a 'common' subsection (Stob. II 41.7–8). The special enquiry considers 'matters pertaining to the individual: such as whether a person who has sense should engage in political activity or live with those capable of leadership, or whether the wise man should marry' (*ibid.* 41.9–11). Eudorus also had a section on lives, of which we are told little except that 'the discussion of marriage was organized as a special part of it, on account of the number of questions raised in it [sc. the discussion of marriage]' (*ibid.* 44.26–45.2).[3]

'Lives' as a topic presumably implies 'choice of lives', and is of course a subject on which most major philosophers from Plato on had much to say.[4] Many like Chrysippus wrote treatises entitled *On Lives* which were doubtless devoted principally to the question of the choice between them, and above all to the issue of whether a wise man should enter politics or be involved with politicians or more generally serve his country, or whether he should rather lead what Chrysippus called the quiet life (ὁ

[2] For orientation on Arius Didymus and the doxographical schemes he presents (and their relation to his own practice), see the collection of essays edited by W.W. Fortenbaugh entitled *On Stoic and Peripatetic Ethics: The Work of Arius Didymus* (New Brunswick, London 1983), and especially D.E. Hahm, 'The Diairetic Method and the Purpose of Arius' Doxography'. Like virtually everyone else who has used M. Giusta, *I dossografi di etica*, 2 vols. (Turin 1964–7), I have been unpersuaded by its highly speculative main theses, but much assisted by the rich store of information it contains.

[3] The prominence of the topic of marriage in these two schemes (Eudorus' especially) is mirrored by its popularity as an example of a political or practical θέσις in the rhetorical handbooks (e.g. Hermogenes *Progymn.* 11, Aphthonius *Progymn.* 13, Theon *Progymn.* 12), with discussion by J. Barns, 'A New Gnomologium: with some remarks on Gnomic Anthologies, II', *CQ* 1 (1951) 1–19, at p. 13, who detects Stoic influence in the phenomenon. On the notion of πολιτικὴ θέσις see the standard monograph of H. Throm, *Die Thesis* (Paderborn 1932), Part II.

[4] There is a useful study by R. Joly, *Le Thème Philosophique des Genres de Vie dans l'Antiquité Classique* (Brussels 1956).

κατὰ τὴν ἡσυχίαν βίος: Plu. *Stoic. rep.* 1043 B) or the leisured life of learning (ὁ σχολαστικὸς βίος: Plu. *Stoic. rep.* 1033 D). On the basis of the doxographical schemes attributed to Philo and Eudorus it seems plausible to conjecture that one favoured way of putting this question about the choice of lives, or alternatively one way of exploring a specific implication of the choice, was to ask: 'Should the wise man marry?' The conjecture is supported by evidence which suggests that in the context of the choice of lives the decision to marry was seen as a decision for the political rather than the quiet life. This evidence is particularly striking in the case of the Stoics, but there are doxographical reports of the views of other philosophers which carry the same implication. Quite what these further reports tell us is a moot point. I shall argue that they reflect the preoccupations of doxography, shaped by Stoic concerns, at least as much as those of the philosophers they purport to represent.

Here are three texts which illustrate the point. None explicitly refers to ' lives' or the choice of lives. But the material they present has surely been assembled with the purpose of demonstrating where the philosophers in question stand on the issue: not only is this the best explanation of their form and content, but in one case there is a parallel text which *does* belong to an explicit discussion of 'lives'. The brief ethical section of the life of Plato in D.L. III 78 contains the following:

> Again, the wise man will take part in politics and marry and not transgress the established laws. As far as is feasible he will also legislate for his own country, unless in a state of excessive corruption of the people he sees things as completely excusing his abstention.

There is a corresponding section in the life of Aristotle (D.L. V 31):

> And the wise man will be a lover and will take part in politics; moreover he will marry and live with a king.

Finally the doxography included in the life of Antisthenes has a similar passage (D.L. VI 11):

> The wise man will take part in politics *not* in accordance with the established laws, but in accordance with the law of virtue. He will marry for the sake of having children, having intercourse with the women of greatest natural endowment. And he will be a lover, for the wise man alone knows whom one should love.

The Aristotle text is condensed[5] from a passage of Arius Didymus (*Stob.* II 143.24–144.15):[6]

> The morally good man will choose a life of virtue, whether he finds himself at some time in a position of leadership, if the needs of the times advance him to it, or whether he has to live with a king or legislate or otherwise take part in politics. If he does not achieve these he will turn to the popular form of life or to the contemplative or to the life of education (which lies as a mean between them). If the needs of the times prevent him from being involved in both [sc. the theoretical and the political life], he will engage in one of the two, preferring the theoretical life, but, because of his capacity for society, throwing himself into political activity. Consequently he will both marry and have children and take part in politics and be a lover (I mean the temperate form of love) and will get drunk at social gatherings, even if not by preference. And in general in the exercise of virtue he will both remain in life and again, if he ever had to do so on account of some constraint, quit it, making provision for his burial in accordance with law and ancestral customs and for the other duties which piety requires us to discharge for the departed.

What Arius Didymus says here makes it clear beyond a doubt that the sentence about Aristotle quoted above from D.L. V 31 relates to the question of the choice of lives, and that the activities it mentions – taking part in politics, becoming a lover, marrying, living with a king – are all conceived of as distinctive of a political life.[7]

[5] Much of the content as well as the distinctive overall structure of D.L. V 31 clearly derives from Arius Didymus (see Stob. II 142.6–145.2); there are elements not present in Stobaeus (e.g. the definition of friendship as 'equality of reciprocal goodwill'), but we cannot determine whether they were in the original Arius Didymus text or whether Diogenes Laertius imports material from another source. Topics follow in the order: non-reciprocity of virtues; passions; love and friendship (but these are reversed in Diogenes Laertius); kindness (χάρις: omitted in Diogenes Laertius); the life of virtue; the three forms of life.

[6] This passage is the subject of an excellent treatment (with critical review of previous studies) in P. Moraux, *Der Aristotelismus bei den Griechen* I (Berlin 1973), pp. 403–18, which illuminates not only the material under immediate consideration but the habits of doxographers more generally.

[7] Later Stoics mount explicit arguments for the proposition that cities could

Some further inferences also seem in order. The trio of texts from Diogenes Laertius just cited makes Plato, Aristotle and Antisthenes address suspiciously similar issues in suspiciously similar terms. They imply that when these philosophers took up the topic of the choice of lives, they approached it with the same questions in mind: Will the wise man take part in politics? Will he respect the established laws or not? Will he be a legislator? Will he be a lover? Will he marry? If so, for what purpose? This already looks like a check list imposed on the exposition by the doxographer in the familiar manner of doxographers, rather than a genuine unanimity of approach on the part of the philosophers in question.[8] Doxographical manipulation is confirmed when we consider the relation between Diogenes Laertius' reports and what we know independently about the political philosophies of Plato and Aristotle. The account of Plato is not only inaccurate but palpably written from a particular point of view, and one not notably close to Plato's own. For example, there is no hint of the utopian framework of the *Republic*. The statement about respect for established laws is a sound enough representation of the *Crito*, but its inclusion becomes more intelligible in the light of the Antisthenes entry: Antisthenes espouses a high-minded antinomianism, Plato still recognizes a framework of public law. Again, while we must bear in mind our ignorance of Aristotle's lost writings, it still seems doubtful that he would have given such prominence in this context to the question of whether the wise man will be a lover or (cf. the longer version in Stobaeus) get drunk.[9]

If the check list of questions and the problematic they reflect are not decidedly Platonic or Aristotelian in emphasis, what *is* their provenance? I answer: Stoic. The answer has to be advanced with due caution. For whereas with Plato and Aristotle we have extensive original texts to compare with Diogenes Laertius' reports, for our knowledge of the Stoics – here as elsewhere – we are heavily dependent on doxographies and other secondary sources, and are consequently less well placed to

not survive without marriage: so e.g. Antipater, *On Marriage*, *ap.* Stob. IV 507.13–508.2; Musonius Rufus, *Is marriage an impediment to philosophizing*?, *ap.* Stob. IV 498.24–499.23. Cf. also e.g. Aphthonius *Progymn.* 13, who writes (49.16–18 Spengel): 'Political questions are those which involve an action which holds the city together, e.g. should one marry? Should one sail? Should one build a fortification? For these are all things which hold a city together if they happen.'

[8] Cf. Moraux, *Der Aristotelismus* I, pp. 410–11.

[9] Cf. Moraux, *Der Aristotelismus* I, pp. 412–13 with n. 300.

detect distortion of Stoic positions in accounts of their views. Nonetheless there is much to be said for the proposition that the check list is essentially a Stoic check list.[10] (1) The questions on it are expressed as questions about the wise man: a Hellenistic if not exclusively Stoic feature. (2) If the list is not Platonic or Aristotelian in inspiration, a Hellenistic origin again seems likeliest. (3) Arguments for thinking that the Antisthenes doxography in D.L. VI 11 represents a Stoic interpretation of his thought were referred to in Chapter 1 above.[11] (4) The interest in whether a wise man will live with a king is one we know Chrysippus in particular concerned himself with: Plutarch attacks his treatment of it and supplies at least one quotation.[12] (5) The only ancient philosophical system we know of which makes the idea that the wise man will be a lover into an important *political* doctrine is Zeno's. It is accordingly plausible that the presence of a question about love on the check list reflects Stoic preoccupations. (6) One might antecedently have thought that the presence of a question about marriage on the list could well reflect principally the disagreement between Plato and Aristotle on the political desirability of the social institution of the family: Plato against marriage, Aristotle in favour of it.[13] But there is no key role for the concept of the sage in such a matrix; and of course the Diogenes Laertius passages put Plato and Aristotle on the same side: the sage *will* marry. According to Diogenes Laertius the thinkers who pronounced against marriage for the wise man were Diogenes the Cynic (VI 72) and Epicurus (X 119). This suggests that the question arose in this particular form in a context where philosophers such as these were advocating withdrawal from contemporary society (Epicurus) or rejection of its norms (Diogenes), and indeed arguing for a decision against 'the political life'. In the same context the Stoics evidently took a firm stand on the opposite side, according to the unanimous testimony of our sources. In maintaining their position they appear to have appealed to what we think of as the Aristotelian principle that man is by nature a social animal. So e.g. Cicero *Fin.* III 68:

[10] This is also Moraux's conclusion, pp. 412–14; cf. Joly, *Genres de Vie*, pp. 151–3.

[11] See p. 11 n. 19.

[12] Plu. *Stoic. rep.* 1043 B–E, 1047 F; *Comm. not.* 1061 D.

[13] Certainly Plato and Aristotle are the thinkers who make marriage an institution of fundamental concern for political philosophy. Its abolition in *Rep.* V and restoration at the beginning of *Pol.* I 2 come immediately to mind. But it is worth also recalling that Plato in the *Laws* gives marriage the kind of primacy in legislation which one might have expected of Aristotle: see *Leg.* 721 A, 772 E ff., 778 BC, 783 D ff..

> Furthermore, since we see that man is born to protect and preserve men, it is in agreement with human nature that men should want to undertake and carry out public duties of state and, in order to live in accordance with nature, take a wife and want children by her. They think that not even love affairs if they are pure are alien to the wise man.

Or again Arius Didymus *apud* Stob. II 109.10–20:

> They say that there are three preferable lives, the kingly, the political, and thirdly the life devoted to knowledge. Likewise there are three preferable ways of acquiring wealth: first from kingship, either by being king oneself or being provided for from the monarch's possessions. Second from political activity, for he [sc. the wise man] will take part in politics in accordance with the account of what is preferable, and in fact (καὶ γάρ) he will marry and have children, since these things follow from the nature of a rational animal designed for community and mutual affection. So he will acquire wealth both from political society and from those of his friends in high places.

Perhaps Epicurus and Diogenes the Cynic would not have rejected the Aristotelian principle in itself; and they both allow the wise man an interest in intercourse with others, whether social (Epicurus) or sexual (Diogenes). What they appear to deny, however, and what the Stoics insist on is that man's social nature generates an altruistic obligation to seek to strengthen the society in which he actually finds himself, by various means including political activity, marriage in accordance with the existing conventions, and the procreation of children. The fullest account of the Stoic position is given in another passage of Arius Didymus. Its philosophical coherence is such as to suggest strongly that the conception of the political life which emerges in all the texts we have been considering owes its definition to Stoicism, even if it is the product of a controversy to which Cynics and Epicureans as well as Stoics were party. Here is the text in question (Stob. II 94.8–20):

> Following on these points is the thesis that the wise man takes part in politics, and especially so in the sorts of political societies which show some progress towards being perfect political societies; also the theses that he legislates and

> that he educates people, and again that it is appropriate for the morally good to compose writings which can benefit those who encounter the writings; also the thesis that he descends[14] both to marriage and to having children, both for himself and for his country, and endures struggles and death for it, if it is a moderate regime. And morally bad things are set alongside these: demagogy, practising as a sophist, composing writings harmful to those who encounter them – which would not befall the morally good.

We are now in a position to consider again the *testimonium* on Zeno at D.L. VII 121:

> They say that the wise man will take part in politics if nothing prevents it, as Chrysippus says in the first book of *On lives*. For he will restrain vice and encourage virtue. He will marry, as Zeno says in the *Republic*, and have children.

As a piece of doxographical information this text must obviously be read as presenting a condensed version of the doctrine spelled out more fully at Stob. II 94.8 ff., with *laudationes* attached to enhance its authority;[15] i.e. it is designed to report Stoic teaching on how the wise man should behave in the political society in which he actually finds himself. Moreover the item on marriage and having children certainly does reproduce the standard Stoic line on the subject.

Did Zeno really originate this line of thought in the *Republic*? The doxographical manhandling of Plato and Aristotle in comparable texts inspires no antecedent confidence in the attribution. Nothing else we are told about the *Republic* (nor, incidentally, about Chrysippus' *On Republic*) concerns the conduct of the sage in existing circumstances. Again, it is interesting that only the point about marriage and having children, not also the ruling on participation in politics, is ascribed to the *Republic*.

[14] This translates συγκαταβαίνειν καὶ εἰς γάμον καὶ εἰς τεκνογονίαν. LSJ s.v. συγκαταβαίνειν makes it apparent that the word in this context carries connotations both of stooping or condescending and of getting oneself into a tricky situation ('walking into it'). Readers of Plato's *Republic* will (rightly or wrongly) be irresistibly reminded of the first symbolic word of the dialogue: κατέβην (327 A), and its resonances in the image of the journey up from the cave and in the subsequent insistence (520 C; cf. 519 D) that the philosopher must once again descend to govern the city: καταβατέον.

[15] I do not imply that Diogenes Laertius himself or his condensing source adds the *laudationes*. The relation of *laudationes* to the doctrines to which they are attached is a difficult and complex issue. For discussion of it as it arises in Book VII see Mansfeld, *Elenchos* 7 (1986) 328–73.

The evidence we have been reviewing makes it hard to doubt that *if* Zeno said there that in existing circumstances the sage should marry, he will have done so in a context of advice on participation in politics and in general on the political life. Why no mention of *that* as a doctrine of the *Republic*?[16]

These arguments – two of them from silence – do not make the most powerful of cases against accepting the attribution of the standard Stoic thesis about marriage and having children to the *Republic*. But if the attribution *is* false (i.e. if option (1) [p. 119] is correct), it is not hard to see how it might erroneously have been made by a doxographer as careless or unscrupulous as the scholar responsible for what is said about Plato at D.L. III 78. As we noted D.L. III 78 simply ignores or forgets Plato's utopianism: it converts Plato's idea of philosopher-kings into a doctrine about the involvement of the wise man in politics in existing circumstances. Perhaps D.L. VII 121 similarly ignores or forgets the utopianism of Zeno's *Republic*, and seizes on its positive interest in relations with women and in having children as showing that Zeno held the doctrine about the sage's choice of the political life in existing circumstances which was to become standard in the school.

[16] Seneca claims that it was Zeno's doctrine that the wise man will enter public affairs unless something prevents it (*de otio* 3, 2). If this is correct, it need not have been the *Republic* in which Zeno formulated the thesis. But it may be that Seneca has simply fathered the general doctrine of the school upon him.

Appendix E

Plato and the Stoics on concord

It is Plato as well as Zeno who makes friendship the key to the well-being of the city (*Alc.* I 126 A–127 D) and Plato as well as (probably) Zeno who defines it in terms of concord (ibid. 126 C, 127 A, C, D; cf. *Rep.* 351 D, *Polit.* 311 B, *Cleit.* 409 E). Now when Plato identifies concord with σωφροσύνη at *Rep.* 432 A, he has already explained it in terms of shared belief (ἡ αὐτὴ δόξα, 431 D; cf. ὁμοδοξία, 433 C), to be subjected to implicit criticism for doing so by Aristotle, who thinks it is too theoretical an account (*EN* IX 6, 1167a22–8); and he glosses 'concord' at once with the further explanation: 'natural harmony (συμφωνία) between worse and better as to which of the two ought to rule both in the city and in one individual' (432 A). It seems very probable that the Stoic material we have been examining effectively accuses Plato of confusing two concepts which ought to be distinguished: concord (ὁμόνοια) and harmony, which – unlike concord – is what is properly defined in terms of shared belief (the Stoics call this ὁμοδογματία, Stob. II 74.4, no doubt in order to avoid a compound of δόξα, as importing connotations of error or weakness (Stob. II 112.2–4; Sextus *M* VII 151) not suggested by δόγμα (cf. J. Barnes, 'The Beliefs of a Pyrrhonist', *PCPS* 208 [1982] 1–30)).

The Stoics were not the first to feel uneasy with Plato's association of concord with shared δόξα. For the author of the *Cleitophon* explicitly raises the question, evidently with the *Republic* in mind (here [409 E] as elsewhere): is concord ὁμοδοξία (cf. *Rep.* 433 C) or knowledge (ἐπιστήμη)? He makes Socrates opt for knowledge, on the ground that friendship (which following *Alc.* I 126 C, 127 C he has defined in terms of concord) is unequivocally a good and the product of justice (cf. *Rep.* 351 D), but ὁμοδοξία sometimes harmful; i.e., he like the Stoics is dissatisfied with the account of concord in Book IV of the *Republic*, because it does not tie concord closely enough to knowledge. (I presently incline to the view that he is *not* Plato, and so find myself more in sympathy with S.R. Slings, *A Commentary on the Platonic Clitophon* (Amsterdam 1981), pp. 253–7 (cf. also H. Thesleff, *Studies in Platonic Chronology* (Helsinki 1982), pp.

205–8), than with e.g. D.L. Roochnik, 'The Riddle of the *Cleitophon*', *Ancient Philosophy* 4 [1984] 132–45.)

There is evidently reason to suppose that the Stoic definition of concord is directly inspired by this passage of the *Cleitophon.* Not only does it canvass the two options – ὁμοδοξία and knowledge – which the Stoics take up in their accounts of harmony and concord, but the *Cleitophon* like the Stoic definition fails to spell out that this knowledge is *shared* knowledge, even though the context makes it clear that shared knowledge is what is in the author's mind. In the *Cleitophon* passage the omission is motivated: the focus is on the question of belief or knowledge, not on the fact that either – whichever concord is – must be shared. The suspicion arises that the Stoics, on the other hand, may have read the passage as giving an account of concord which needed to be completed only by the specification of the goods that are the object of knowledge as common goods (this specification would presumably have enabled Socrates to avoid Cleitophon's objection, 410 A). Such a reading would lack something in philosophical intelligence, but might have been thought to have the merit of faithfulness to an authoritative text – if, that is, the *Cleitophon* were construed as an authoritative retraction by Plato himself of the treatment of concord in the *Republic.* There is good reason to think that Chrysippus knew the *Cleitophon* and regarded it as by Plato: see Plu. *Stoic. rep.* 1039 DE with *Cleit.* 408 A, discussed e.g. by R. Westman, 'Chrysipp III 761 und der Dialog Kleitophon', *Eranos* 59 (1961) 89–100, and Slings, *A Commentary on the Platonic Clitophon*, pp. 240–2.

Appendix F

Cleanthes' syllogism

Besides the official Stoic definition of *city* preserved in Clement and Dio there is in Arius Didymus a passage which appears to contain another, attributed to Cleanthes. The text in question is an argument quoted by Arius Didymus as constituting a proof of the Stoic thesis that the city is morally good (σπουδαῖον). Its first premiss is naturally read as a definition. The Greek as preserved in the MSS reads as follows (Stob. II 103.14–17):

> πόλις μὲν ἔστιν οἰκήτηριον κατασκεύασμα εἰς ὃ καταφεύγοντας ἔστι δίκην δοῦναι καὶ λαβεῖν· οὐκ ἀστεῖον δὴ πόλις ἐστίν; ἀλλὰ μὴν τοιοῦτόν ἐστιν ἡ πόλις οἰκητήριον· ἀστεῖον ἄρ' ἔστιν ἡ πόλις.

It is generally agreed that the text as thus transmitted is corrupt: the final two clauses look like the minor premiss and the conclusion of a syllogism, but there is no appropriate major premiss to launch the syllogism. It has also been generally supposed that the problem can easily be solved by inserting εἰ with Heeren after μέν. A translation might then run:

> If a city is a habitable construction to which people may have recourse for the dispensation of justice, then a city is surely refined.
> But a city is that sort of habitation.
> So a city is refined.

The syllogism so derived is puzzling in a variety of ways. The protasis of the conditional premiss, however, could reasonably be construed as a definition of *city*.

There are grounds for thinking that the corruption goes deeper than that, perhaps much deeper. Even with Heeren's supplement οἰκητήριον remains problematical. In the major premiss it figures as an adjective, in the minor as a noun, apparently with the implication that it functioned the same way in the major (τοιοῦτον would naturally pick up an *adjectival* phrase qualifying οἰκητήριον there). If there were no other reason to suspect the text, this difficulty might be put down simply to clumsiness on Cleanthes' part. Given that we already know it to be in need of emendation, it is tempting to conjecture further corruption. Modest suggestions might be that κατασκεύασμα is a gloss (not a clever gloss) on οἰκητήριον (the noun) which has crept into the text, or that (as Jaap Mansfeld puts to me as a possibility) it originally read κατεσκευασμένον – a 'properly equipped' habitation. Emendation along these lines would improve not just the Greek of the passage but also its sense. There seems no reason whatever why Cleanthes should wish to talk of the city as a *building* or a *construction* in this context. What his argument requires is *only* that he fasten attention on some moral or social property of cities.

The moral property which the text makes him introduce is itself odd in the context. Is Cleanthes talking about cities as they ideally are? One would have expected him to be doing so, given that his object (as interpreted by Arius Didymus) is to prove the city a thing of moral excellence. But in Zeno's city of sages there are no law courts, presumably (among other reasons) because there is no injustice and no need for the dispensation of legal justice. So why does Cleanthes pick on dispensation of justice as the key moral characteristic of the city?

This leads me to doubt the credentials of the whole clause κατασκεύασμα εἰς ὃ καταφεύγοντας ἔστι δίκην δοῦναι καὶ λαβεῖν. Taken just on its own, of course, this phrase would provide an apt definition not of *city* but of *law-court:* which prompts the guess that at some stage in the transmission οἰκητήριον (not the commonest of words) was misread as or taken to be an error for δικαστήριον by a scribe who added the words κατασκεύασμα... λαβεῖν as an explanatory gloss, later incorporated into the text.

If we excise them, we need an appropriate epithet to qualify οἰκητήριον. *Exempli gratia* I suggest that Cleanthes originally wrote: ΠΟΛΙΣΕΙΕΝΝΟΜΟΝΕΣΤΙΝΟΙΚΗΤΗΡΙΟΝ, 'if a city is a law-governed habitation'. Corruption to ΠΟΛΙΣΜΕΝΕΣΤΙΝΟΙΚΗΤΗΡΙΟΝ is palaeographically plausible: the errant scribe's eye skips a sequence mostly of Ε, Ν, Ο, substituting an Ε for an Ο when he picks up the thread again. Moreover, there are a number of more substantive grounds for making this sort of conjecture about what Cleanthes really said.

First, immediately after quoting the syllogism Arius Didymus writes as follows (Stob. II 103.17–23):

> But 'city' is said in three ways: one referring to a habitation, one referring to an organization of people (men,

> ἀνθρώπων), the third referring to both of these. In two senses the city is called refined – when it refers to an organization of people and when it refers to both of these (because of the reference to the inhabitants).

Arius Didymus' source evidently quoted Cleanthes' argument along with a commentary on it. And the commentary is plainly critical, even though the syllogism is introduced with the remark: 'In fact Cleanthes put forward an argument which deals adequately with the proposition that the city is morally good'. For the effect of the commentator's distinctions is to point out that of the three senses of 'city', it is the other two, not the one Cleanthes focuses on, which are appropriate to the thesis that the city exhibits refinement.

But while the commentator is unhappy with 'habitation' in Cleanthes' premiss, he is likely enough to have been content with the epithet Cleanthes employed there to characterize the crucial moral property of the city. For he does not criticize *that* (so far as we are told); and it seems not improbable that the commendation of the syllogism for 'adequacy' is due to him. If so, the epithet in question has a good chance of being 'law-governed', since (i) the commentator appears to allude to the standard Stoic definition when he talks of the city as an 'organization of people (σύστημα ἀνθρώπων)', and (ii) in that definition the 'organization or group' of people which constitutes a city is said to be 'administered by law'.

Second, Cleanthes' syllogism must be supposed to stand in some sort of dialectical relation with an argument recorded by Diogenes Laertius (VI 72), and ascribed to Diogenes the Cynic:

> With regard to the law he held that it is impossible for there to be political government without it. For he says:
>
> (1) Without a city there is no profit in refinement (ἀστείου); and the city is refined.
> (2) Without law there is no profit in a city.
> (3) So the law is refined.

Diogenes' argument is itself the subject of intricate scholarly controversy.[1] For present purposes I will summarize my view of its status

[1] For surveys and discussions of the controversy see M.-O. Goulet-Cazé, 'Un syllogisme stoïcien sur la loi dans la doxographie de Diogène le Cynique à propos de Diogène Laërce VI 72', *Rhein. Mus.* 125 (1982) 214–40, and G. Giannantoni, *Socraticorum Reliquiae* (Naples 1985), III 487–8.

and object as a preface to consideration of its relationship with Cleanthes' argument.

Briefly, then, the quoted passage belongs to the doxographical section (VI 70–3) in the life of Diogenes. This section, although not derived from a unique source, throughout presents material that has been heavily Stoicized.[2] Within it VI 72 as a whole constitutes an attempt to make Diogenes a constructive political philosopher of a proto-Stoic cast.[3] It is best explained on the supposition that genuine Diogenean sayings have been converted into theoretical positions they were never designed to express. For example, Diogenes' famous claim (VI 63) to be κοσμοπολίτης, 'citizen of the universe', is turned into the thesis that 'the only correct constitution is the one in the universe'. Other evidence about the early Cynics suggests that what Diogenes meant was that the only place where he really belonged was the universe itself. 'Belonging' is the sole element in the connotation of 'citizen' that is exploited positively, not any implication of a community or a constitution.

In the present instance it appears that both original saying and Stoicizing gloss are preserved together.[4] First we are given a bit of bland theorizing: political government, or a political constitution, is impossible without law. The implication seems to be that Diogenes advocated the doctrine of the rule of law. Yet if one thing is clear about early Cynicism it is that the sources regularly associate it with emphatic *rejection* of νόμος

[2] Harmonization of Cynic and Stoic positions in Diogenes Laertius is discussed in general by J. Mansfeld, 'Diogenes Laertius on Stoic philosophy', *Elenchos* 7 (1986) 296–382, at pp. 317–351. For the Stoicization in VI 70–1 see the largely convincing treatment by M.-O. Goulet-Cazé, *L'Ascèse Cynique* (Paris 1986), with Mansfeld's critical comments (*CR* 38 (1988) 162–3). She shows that the principal doctrine of the passage, 'la double ascèse', is a teaching of the Stoics of the Imperial era, particularly of Musonius Rufus, and is unlikely to be truly Diogenean.

[3] See Appendix H for a more detailed discussion of this point.

[4] Goulet-Cazé, 'Un syllogisme stoïcien', *Rh. Mus.* 125 (1982) 214–40, argues that the Stoic parallels, and especially Cleanthes' syllogism, indicate that the argument ascribed to Diogenes is itself really a Stoic argument: Diogenes never advanced any such train of reasoning. This is implausible. The explanations Goulet-Cazé advances of how and why it wrongly got attributed to Diogenes are too speculative to carry conviction (*ibid.*, pp. 232–40). Her position is also founded on a dubious assumption: that ἀστεῖον in this context means 'morally good' or 'morally refined', although as Goulet-Cazé acknowledges (*ibid.*, p. 223 n.26) most scholars have preferred 'urbanum', 'civilised', *vel sim.* If the moral interpretation of ἀστεῖον were right, then the first premiss of the argument would indeed express a thought uncharacteristic of Cynicism, viz. that there is no profit in moral goodness apart from the city. Appendix G will show, however, that the majority view about what ἀστεῖον means here is probably correct.

and the city. Presumably the Stoicizing doxographer who attributes the doctrine to Diogenes thought that the argument he goes on to quote gives him adequate grounds nonetheless for the attribution. But the argument more naturally invites an alternative construal. I guess that Diogenes has in his sights an opponent who concedes (cf. premiss (1)) that refinement of manners is a city phenomenon which is thoroughly unnatural and so ethically worthless. Diogenes' object will then have been to show him that in that case he must also concede something which he does *not* wish to allow (cf. the conclusion (3)): that law, too, is unnatural and without value, for it too exhibits refinement. In short, Diogenes' argument is – as one would expect – *antinomian*, directed against those who sympathize with his aversion to the city and its manners, but who hold to the view rejected by him that the rule of law is indispensable.

We are now in a position to return to Cleanthes. Whatever the right version of the text of his syllogism may have been, (a) he is arguing that the city is refined; (b) the point of the argument must be to reply somehow to Diogenes; (c) in Cleanthes' hands the thesis specified in (a) has a positive resonance – unlike Diogenes he takes refinement to be a morally excellent thing. On the version of Cleanthes' text I have proposed the syllogism has a beautifully apt and clear anti-Diogenean point it would otherwise lack. Diogenes argues from the unacceptable refinement of the city to the unacceptable refinement of law.[5] Cleanthes turns this reasoning on its head: the city has the virtue of being law-governed (see e.g. his *Hymn to Zeus* for exposition of the fundamental role and value of law in the Stoic system); and if it has this virtue, it *thereby* has the virtue of refinement – refinement in the proper and morally acceptable sense of the word. It is as though Cleanthes is saying: Diogenes is right to see a connection between law and refinement, but he has the connection quite the wrong way round.[6]

There is further indirect support for the idea that Cleanthes (and indeed the early Stoics in general) effectively defined refinement in terms of law. Immediately after quoting his syllogism and the three definitions of *city* (Stob. II 103.12–23), Arius Didymus reports (*ibid.* 103.24–104.1):

[5] The inference is, of course, invalid. One may agree to both (1) and (2) of Diogenes' argument but reject his conclusion (3). The point could be demonstrated formally, but it is briefer to note that the reason why cities are unprofitable without law need not (and indeed does not) have anything to do with their refinement.

[6] For this idea about the relation of Cleanthes' and Diogenes' arguments I am indebted to Myles Burnyeat.

> They say that every wicked man is also rustic. For rusticity is inexperience of the practices and laws in a city: of which every wicked man is guilty.

If rusticity or boorishness (ἀγροικία) is inexperience of law in the city, must not refinement or urbanity by the same token be *experience* of law in the city?[7]

[7] I develop further in Appendix G the suggestions made in this paragraph.

Appendix G

ἀστεῖον

The word rendered as 'exhibiting refinement' (ἀστεῖον) has a core literal sense of 'urban'. So, as Long and Sedley note, commenting on Cleanthes' syllogism, some punning seems to be going on: the city might be expected to be refined just because it is urban.[1] In their englishing of the syllogism they translate 'civilized', which has the merit of suggesting both refinement and the civic.[2] But there is a drawback to 'civilized'. In Greek literature of the fifth and fourth centuries B.C. ἀστεῖος is a word applied to people (e.g. 'urbane'), their persons (e.g. 'neat'), behaviour (e.g. 'refined'), and especially their mode of speech ('refined', 'polite', sometimes 'witty').[3] It is not an expression used to describe an institution or a society, and if it were, one would expect it to imply something about manners rather than political and moral function, which is what Cleanthes in the major premiss makes it turn upon. 'Civilized' *is* a term which can hit off the moral quality of a society, but for that very reason its employment here rather muffles the shock which Cleanthes' use of ἀστεῖος administers. There is yet a further complication. In many doxographical texts ἀστεῖον is effectively a synonym of σπουδαῖον, 'morally good', a usage going back to Chrysippus at any rate; and it is not at all obvious that much of the force 'civilized', 'refined' remains live in such contexts.

Although some scholars would deny it, there can be no doubt that 'refined', not 'morally good', is the right rendering of the word as it appears in the reasoning (discussed in Appendix F) ascribed to Diogenes of Sinope (D.L. VI 72):

[1] A.A. Long and D.N. Sedley, *The Hellenistic Philosophers* (Cambridge 1987) II 425.

[2] *Ibid.* I 431.

[3] For bibliographical information and especially access to a copy of Lammermann, as well as for discussion of the usage of the expression (and of *urbanum, urbanitas*, etc.), I am indebted to John Procopé. Besides LSJ s.v. ἀστεῖος see above all the dissertation of K. Lammermann, *Von der attischen Urbanität und ihrer Auswirkung in der Sprache* (Göttingen 1935), which does for ἀστεῖος what O. Ribbeck had done for ἄγροικος in *Agroikos*, Abhandl. der phil.-hist. Kl. der Kgl. Sächs. Ges. d. Wiss. 10 (1888).

(1) Without a city there is no profit in refinement (ἀστείου); and the city is refined.
(2) Without law there is no profit in a city.
(3) So the law is refined.

(1) is much more obviously plausible if ἀστεῖον is taken as 'refined'. Refinement in the country might well seem pointless – the rustics will not appreciate it. Or if 'city' here signifies more broadly 'civil society', not just the town, refinement of manners will again be pointless, since manners are an essentially social phenomenon. On the other hand, the idea that being morally good is pointless apart from civil society has much less intuitive appeal. Of course, Antiphon the sophist or an adherent of the Hobbeist contract theory of justice presented by Glaucon in *Republic* II might put arguments in support of the idea. But it would certainly need arguing; and it is hard to think of any philosophy less likely to want to argue it than Cynicism. For Cynics moral goodness is necessary for happiness and self-sufficiency, regardless of the demands and rewards of civil society.

Appendix F has suggested that in his syllogism on the city Cleanthes offers a riposte to Diogenes' argument, and turns ἀστεῖον from a pejorative epithet describing manners into a term of moral approbation tied to the notion of obedience to law, although still *meaning* 'refined'. I call this Stage 1 in the history of the word. This interpretation was supported by reference to the account Arius Didymus goes on to give of rusticity after reporting the syllogism. The passage in question runs as follows (Stob. II 103.24–104.9):

> They say that every wicked man is also rustic. For rusticity is inexperience of the practices and laws in a city: of which every wicked man is guilty. He is also savage, since he is in extreme opposition to a way of life in accordance with law, and bestial, and given to harming men. And this same person is both wild and tyrannical, being so disposed as to act depotically, and moreover cruelly and violently and lawlessly, seizing his opportunities. And he is also ungrateful, not having the appropriate (οἰκείως) attitude to the return of favours nor to distributing them, because he does nothing in a spirit of community or friendship or spontaneity.

This text indeed supplies indirect but powerful confirmation that there was a time in the history of the early Stoa when ἀστεῖον was not a mere synonym of σπουδαῖον, 'morally good', but meant 'refined', which was interpreted as 'subject to law' or something similar. For the idea that the wicked are 'rustic' only makes much sense if it complements the idea that the good or wise are refined. And the interpretation of refined as governed by law is supported by the explanations given of the attributes of the wicked. The wicked man is an exile because he is bereft of law, rustic or boorish because he has no familiarity with the laws of the city, savage because his way of life is the very opposite of one lived in accordance with law, tyrannical because he is disposed to act lawlessly.

Arius Didymus tells us that Cleanthes' syllogism was designed to establish not only that the city is refined, but that it is morally good (σπουδαῖον). For him ἀστεῖον just means 'morally good', even though in the argument he is commenting on it should actually be understood as 'refined', if I am right in connecting Cleanthes' syllogism closely with the argument ascribed to Diogenes in D.L. VI 72. It is not difficult to see how this further transformation in the meaning of the word – I call it Stage 2 – must have come about. Stoicism is solely responsible. For the Stoics the refined man, as opposed to the boor, is the law-governed man. But Stoicism effects a radical transformation in the concept of law: it is not the set of statutes and customs which men in any given community have worked out to govern their common life, but the internal voice of reason prescribing to each and every person, wherever he or she lives, what should or should not be done. Thus the only man who truly lets law govern his life is the one who obeys right reason consistently. And he is the good man – good because he is wise. Therefore to be refined comes to the same thing as being good. Refinement is no longer one among the moral virtues. Because being refined is just the consistent disposition to follow the law, which is the moral law, it is simply the same as goodness or moral virtue. The word ἀστεῖος is set to become an ethical term of utmost generality, convertible with σπουδαῖος, 'morally good'.[4]

It might be asked: given that the Stoics made so many properties, from kingship and freedom to wealth and ruggedness (αὐστηρός), functions of moral goodness, and regulated vocabulary accordingly, why of all these regimented expressions did ἀστεῖος come to express moral goodness *in general*? The answer is presumably that on the Stoic view there was no content to refinement other than obedience to law, and obedience to law (i.e. to right reason) is what moral goodness consists in. By contrast a notion like kingship retains its traditional specific sense of ἀρχὴ ἀνυπεύθυνος, unaccountable rule (cf. Herod. III 80.3, Pl. *Leg.* 761 E, *Def.* 415 B, Ar. *Pol.* 1295a20, Diod. I 70.1, Dio Chrys. III 5, LVI 5, 11): the Stoics argue that only the wise man is, properly speaking, someone who does not need scrutiny, for he has knowledge of good and bad (D.L. VII 122). Their account of freedom, as the power of autonomous action (D.L. VII 121), is not similarly traditional (although doubtless it is meant to capture something speakers of

Chrysippus himself was probably the first to use the two words interchangeably, as is suggested e.g. by a quotation, probably from his *On Right Actions*, in Plu. *Stoic. rep.* 1038 A:[5]

> In the same way nothing is alien to the ἀστεῖος, nothing is his own concern for the wicked.

Nor is it surprising that the use of ἀστεῖον to mean 'morally good' in due course made its presence felt in the interpretation of the Diogenean argument D.L. VI 72. Witness the following passage from Cicero's *De Legibus* (II 12):

> *M.* I put a question to you, Quintus, as they [sc. the philosophers] are in the habit of doing: supposing the state were to be without something such that it would have to be considered worth nothing for this very reason that it is without it – is that thing to be counted among the goods?
> *Q.* Yes, one of the greatest goods.
> *M.* If a state is without law, does it have to be considered of no value for that reason?
> *Q.* That cannot be denied.
> *M.* It is necessary, therefore, for law to be considered one of the greatest goods.
> *Q.* I agree entirely.

As Marie-Odile Goulet-Cazé has pointed out,[6] Cicero is here reproducing a version of Diogenes' reasoning, or rather of the inference from

(2) Without law there is no profit in a city

Greek in general would have agreed to be an important element in the connotation of the word). But once again they leave the expression with a highly specific content. And so with the vast majority of the terms they commandeer.

[5] Cf. *Stoic. rep.* 1043 A. An important piece of evidence is D.L. VII 199, where in the catalogue of Chrysippus' writings the following three successive titles are recorded:

> Definitions of the ἀστεῖον, to Metrodorus (2 books)
> Definitions of the morally bad (φαῦλον), to Metrodorus (2 books)
> Definitions of the intermediates (ἀνάμεσα), to Metrodorus (2 books)

The first title on its own might suggest the speculation that Chrysippus himself discussed the sorts of differences in the usage of ἀστεῖον examined in this Appendix. But taken in context the word is clearly just equivalent to σπουδαῖον, 'morally good'.

[6] 'Un syllogisme stoïcien', *Rh. Mus.* 125 (1982) 211–40, at pp. 222–3.

to

(3) So the law is ἀστεῖον.

He attributes the argument to 'the philosophers', i.e. the Stoics; and as well as helping us to clear up a syntactic ambiguity in the Greek text of (2)[7] he thereby supplies further reason to think that the argument was discussed in the Stoa, even if it was not a Stoic argument. But in Cicero's version, or rather in the Greek source on which he draws, ἀστεῖον is read as 'morally good', not as 'refined', as in the original version. It is of course an entirely natural reading, indeed so natural that Cicero's source probably did not even realize that an alternative construal was – or had once been – available. Certainly it is the thesis that law is good, not that it is refined, which is conveyed by the claim that it is ἀστεῖον in the Stoic doxography (Stob. II 96.10–17; cf. 102.4–10).

[7] As is further argued by Goulet-Cazé, *ibid.*, pp. 221–3. The Greek reads: νόμου δὲ ἄνευ πόλεως οὐδὲν ὄφελος. Scholars have often taken ἄνευ with πόλεως, not νόμου (so e.g. the Loeb, Gigante), no doubt influenced by ἄνευ πόλεως in premiss (1). This yields

(2′) Without a city there is no profit in law.

(2′) is then *parallel* to

(1a) Without a city there is no profit in refinement.

But in that case one would expect as conclusion not

(3) The law is refined

but

(3′) The city is law-governed,

to run parallel with

(1b) The city is refined.

Appendix H

Diogenes' cosmopolitanism (D.L. VI 72)

Here is D.L. VI 72 in translation:

(a) He said that all things belong to the wise, putting the sort of argument we cited above [VI 37]:

> All things belong to the gods.
> The gods are friends of the wise.
> The possessions of friends are held in common.

(b) With regard to the law he held that it is impossible for there to be political government without it. For he says:

> Without a city there is no profit in refinement;
>   and the city is refined.
> Without law there is no profit in a city.
> So the law is refined.

(c) He would ridicule good birth and fame and all those sorts of things, saying that they were the ornaments of vice. And (d) he said that the only correct constitution was the one in the universe. (e) He said that women should be held in common, recognizing no convention of marriage, but taking the view that a man and a woman should have sex with each other provided only that they persuade each other. And for this reason he thought that sons too should be held in common.

It is worth quoting also the beginning of the next paragraph (VI 73):

> He held that there was nothing out of place in taking something out of a temple or in eating the flesh of any animal; nor even anything unholy in tasting human flesh, as was clear from foreign customs.

There follows an account of Diogenes' adherence to an Anaxagorean theory of the presence of all substances in all (attributed to his tragedy

Thyestes). This is evidently produced to indicate the physical justification offered for the ethics of cannibalism. The paragraph, and with it the doxographical section, ends with a report of Diogenes' rejection of the value of the study of music, geometry, astronomy, etc..

The sequence of items (a)–(e) is not arbitrary. Compare the similar sequence in the doxographical summary of Antisthenes' philosophy at D.L. VI 10–11 (what follows is from VI 11):

> (a') He held that the wise man is self-sufficient, for the possessions of everyone else all belong to him; (c') that ill repute is a good thing and equivalent to suffering (πόνος); (b'/d') that the wise man will engage in politics in accordance not with the established laws, but with the law of virtue; (e') that he will marry for the sake of having children, having sex with the women of highest natural endowment; (f') and that he will love, for only the wise man knows whom one should love.

This list of Antisthenean doctrines is preceded by an account of his general theory of virtue and its acquisition, just as D.L. VI 72 follows an account of Diogenes' views on virtue and its acquisition.

The expository scheme organizing the material in the two passages seems to be the following:

(1) Virtue and its acquisition
(2) Goods – possessed by / common to the wise
(3) True and false goods – discussion of wealth, reputation, good birth
(4) Law and political activity
(5) Marriage

No surviving presentation of Stoic ethics follows this scheme so faithfully, but there are sequences in Stobaeus and D.L. VII which look very much like extracts from larger wholes organized according to the principles of the scheme. Thus in Stobaeus we have: [S1] II 98.14–101.4 – virtue, and the account of the morally good and morally bad man; [S3] II 101.5–20 – the only goods are virtue or what participates in virtue, although *true* wealth and *true* virtue are goods; [S2] II 101.21–102.3 – all goods are common to the morally good; [S4] 102.4–104.9 – accounts of law and the city, of those who obey law or are deprived it, of the morally good man's title to rule. Some of the material we considered in Appendix D is relevant in this connection. At Stobaeus II 93.19–94.20 we have

[S12] II 93.19–94.6 – all goods are common to the morally good, who are in concord with one another; [S14] II 94.8ff. – political activity of the wise man; [S15] II 94.14–17 – he marries and has children. D.L. VII 121 contains [DL4] – political activity of the wise man, [DL5] – he marries and has children; and finally information about his acting the Cynic, including the detail that he will taste human flesh if circumstances dictate it. Compare D.L. VI 72–3, which makes the account of Diogenes' endorsement of cannibalism follow that of his position on marriage.

There is a natural conclusion to draw from these striking similarities in structure and indeed in substance between accounts of Cynic and Stoic ethics: the doxographies of Antisthenes and Diogenes in D.L. VI are designed to present them as philosophizing in very much the same way as the Stoics. Compare the treatment of Plato and Aristotle in D.L. III and V (examined in Appendix D), and indeed of the Cyrenaic Theodorus (D.L. II 98–9), to whom are ascribed in immediate succession the Cynic views that the universe is our native country and that the morally good man will engage in theft, adultery and temple-robbing at the right time.

Scholars have sometimes connected the report ((d) above) that 'the only correct constitution was the one in the universe' with Philodemus' assertion (*On the Stoics* col. XX 4–6) that 'it is their view [sc. that of the Stoics and Cynics] that we should not think any of the cities or laws we know to be a city or a law'. But there is strong reason to suspect that the attribution to Diogenes of a doctrine about the only correct constitution is a heavily Stoicized 'interpretation' of some such remark as the famous claim to be κοσμοπολίτης (D.L. VI 63). For as Clement reports (*Strom.* IV 26, *SVF* III 327):

> The Stoics say that the universe (οὐρανός) is in the proper sense a city, but that those here on earth are not – they are called cities, but are not really.

The similar Stoic conception of the universe as a city common to men and gods is familiar from the texts discussed in Chapter 3, as also from Philo (e.g. *op. mund.* 142–3), who connects it with the notion of the κοσμοπολίτης. The complementary criticism of existing laws and constitutions is likewise found elsewhere in the evidence for Stoicism, in Diogenianus' attack on Chrysippus for departing from the common notions to which he pays lip service (Euseb. *praep. ev.* VI p. 264b, *SVF* III 324):

> How is it that you say that all laws which have been posited and all constitutions are in error?

Philodemus' evidence is naturally taken as implying that existing laws and societies fall short of a positive ideal. But is it good information about Diogenes? It comes from a section of *On the Stoics* where, having established that Zeno's *Republic* is true Zeno and Diogenes' *Republic* really by Diogenes, Philodemus begins (col. XVIII 1–2):

> Let us now write down the noble doctrines held by these people.

A litany of horrid beliefs, mostly about the propriety of indecent sexual practices, follows. Philodemus presumably means us to believe that we could find any of them either in Zeno's book or in Diogenes'. Could we have done? Has he read both books and found them all in both of them? Probably Philodemus relies throughout his tract on other writers for his testimony on Zeno and Diogenes. There is certainly no evidence that he has seen Diogenes' book himself. In any event, the material he presents in this section of his work corresponds so closely (for example) with the material Sextus assembles to discredit Zeno and Chrysippus in *PH* III 245–8 and *M* XI 190–4, and otherwise with Cassius' evidence on Zeno's *Republic*, that it is unsafe in the extreme to suppose that anything not otherwise attested as solidly Cynic goes back to Diogenes. The remark about cities and laws is a case in point. It expresses in similar language the same doctrine as Diogenianus ascribes to Chrysippus. The reasonable conclusion to draw is that it derives (no doubt *via* some doxographical source) from Chrysippus, not Diogenes. It is a conclusion which entails that Philodemus is rather unscrupulous in his polemical tactics. The surprise would be if he were not.

The anecdotal tradition assures us that Diogenes used to describe himself, quoting tragedy, as (D.L. VI 38):

> Citiless, homeless, without a country,
> A beggar, a wanderer, living life from day to day.

This gives us the clue to the proper interpretation of the κοσμοπολίτης quip. What it communicates is (in Goulet-Cazé's words) 'un cosmopolitisme négatif'. The same style of thought is evident in a saying attributed to Crates (D.L. VI 93):

> He said that ignominy and poverty were his country, which Fortune could not take captive, and that Diogenes was his city, which Envy could not plot against.

(Διογένους ... πολίτης is usually translated 'a fellow-citizen of Diogenes' (Loeb) or 'aveva ... come concittadino Diogene' (Gigante), but this misses the symmetry of the two remarks which make up the aphorism.) Along similar lines is a passage alleged to come from one of Crates' tragedies (D.L. VI 98):

My country is not one tower, one roof,
But the whole earth is a citadel and home
Ready for us to spend our life in.

Epilogue

'Impossible hypotheses'

At about the time *The Stoic Idea of the City* was first published, I remember giving an account of the book to my senior colleague Harry Hinsley (1918–98), who was a distinguished historian of international relations, although rather more famous for his role in the World War II code-breaking operation which deciphered Enigma. Hinsley heard me without comment. But he believed the most effective means yet devised by man of sustaining a peaceful international order had been the nuclear balance of terror. The Stoics' rationalist faith in virtue, love and friendship was probably striking him – I thought to myself – as a distant precursor of those unworkable paradigms devised by philosophers and political thinkers in the early modern period which he had studied in the opening chapters of *Power and the Pursuit of Peace.*[1]

Zeno's *Republic* was already regarded as incorrigibly utopian in classical antiquity. Plutarch speaks of Zeno as 'modelling a sort of dream or image of a philosopher's idea of good government and political order' (see Appendix A). Philodemus records among other complaints about the work the charge that 'his legislation consisted of impossible hypotheses for people who don't exist – disregarding those who do' (*On the Stoics* col. XII 8–11). The point here was presumably that (1) Zeno's city was envisaged as a community of the virtuous and wise, and (2) the Stoics themselves conceded (so it was thought) that good men are rarer than the Ethiopian phoenix (e.g. Seneca *Ep.* 42.1, Alex. *Fat.* 199.14–22). It could accordingly be argued (3) that Zeno's project was in effect a purely hypothetical exercise whose basic assumption (1) was all

1 F.H. Hinsley, *Power and the Pursuit of Peace* (Cambridge 1963).

but unrealisable (on account of (2)).[2] In our time the argument has been pushed further: from (2) we can conclude (3′) that Zeno must actually have *conceived* of his good city as an unattainable ideal.[3]

But there is little reason to accept the truth of (3′). Philodemus also reports that Zeno at the very beginning of the *Republic* represented himself as offering 'something applicable to the places in which he found himself and the times in which he lived' (*On the Stoics* col. XII 2–6).[4] Zeno's words have the air of polemic. And the target is scarcely in doubt. It is Plato in his *Republic* who has Socrates stress the difficulties in realising *his* scheme for an ideal city, but insist nonetheless that it will come or that it has come into existence – at some point in the future or in the infinity of past time, or even now in some foreign place far beyond our ken (*Rep.* VI 499 C–D). Zeno is saying: the community described in *my Republic,* unlike the one in Plato's, is achievable *both* here *and* in the present. It is not difficult to see why he thought the claim reasonable. In Zeno's city there is no legislation, no eugenic programme,

[2] Whether the alleged impossibility of Zeno's 'hypotheses' turned on anything other than the difficulty of finding wise and virtuous persons to satisfy them is unclear. Perhaps (for example) the idea that sexual communism would promote love and harmony in society (D.L. VII 131) struck some as incompatible with human nature, as the similar arrangements proposed by Plato in his *Republic* similarly struck Aristotle (*Pol.* II 3–4).

[3] So e.g. D. Dawson, *Cities of the Gods* (New York and Oxford 1992), Ch. 4, esp. pp. 165–6. My article 'Zeno of Citium's anti-utopianism', *Polis* 15.1–2 (1998) 139–49, is a review of Dawson's book; an expanded version has now appeared in my book *Saving the City* (London 1999). It contains some second thoughts on topics explored in the present work.

[4] The passage as a whole (col. XII 1–20) runs as follows (I offer conjectures – in square brackets – on the missing beginning and on references of anaphoric pronouns etc.): '[Zeno's defenders go astray when they say he didn't mind] whether it [sc. his *politeia*] were to come into being, overlooking that at the beginning of the composition he makes it clear that he presents it [sc. his *politeia*] as something applicable to the places in which he found himself and to the times in which he lived. And [sc. they also go astray] because it would be something that deserved to attract censure if he *had* made it that [sc. just a dream]. And inasmuch as his legislation consisted of hypotheses that were once again [sc. just like Plato's] impossible, for people who don't exist – disregarding those who do. And because given that as his project was as described [sc. an exhortation to virtue], someone who then hypothesised such sacrilegious hypotheses was a wretch. And as to the rest of the book, that on whatever topic one takes there is no excess of impiety he has left untouched. And finally that in other works, too, he proposes similar legislation.'

no stratification of society or military organisation, and so no need for the absolute powers of a philosopher ruler – a ruler likely to be found only in some time or at some place far distant from now or here. All that is necessary for the realisation of Zeno's vision is that people begin to exercise their capacity for virtue: a strenuous undertaking, but something wholly within their own power right here and now. To put the point more crisply, Zeno's message in the *Republic* is perhaps best construed as an injunction: make your own city, with your own friends, now, wherever you happen to live.

Such a message is just what we might have expected – except for the heavy emphasis on friendship and community – from a philosopher with as strong a Cynic pedigree as Zeno's; and as Chapter I demonstrates, his *Republic* was perceived in antiquity with some justice as a thoroughly Cynic manifesto. Here it is worth noting a passage at the end of Diogenes Laertius' book on the Cynics, following his assertion of a close relationship between Cynicism and Stoicism: 'Hence it has been said that Cynicism is a short cut to virtue;[5] and in this style [i.e. the Cynic] Zeno of Citium too lived his life' (D.L. VI 104). The claim about Zeno's lifestyle is confirmed by the evidence in the biographical tradition on which Diogenes Laertius draws in the early sections of Book VII (1–31). Although on this account Zeno did not drop out of society in the theatrical manner of a Diogenes of Sinope, he does seem to have cultivated a Cynicising persona of poverty, frugality, general brusqueness, and incivility to kings and their ambassadors in particular.[6]

5 A remark elsewhere attributed to the *Ethics* of Apollodorus, a Stoic of the second century B.C. (D.L. VII 121).

6 See in particular Timon's abuse of his students and associates as 'exceptionally beggarly' (D.L. VII 16) and the verses about Zeno preserved at D.L. VII 27: hexameters which ascribe to him a combination of physical stamina and philosophical single-mindedness reminiscent of Socrates (cf. *Symp.* 219 D–221 C), and trimeters of a more Cynic cast from a drama probably by Philemon, an Athenian comic playwright who was (like Timon) his contemporary. On this material and other evidence for Zeno's public persona see F. Decleva Caizzi, 'The Porch and the Garden: early Hellenistic images of the philosophical life', in *Images and Ideologies: Self-Definition in the Hellenistic World,* ed. A.W. Bulloch, E.S. Gruen, A.A. Long and A. Stewart (Berkeley 1993) 303–29. But see also J. Brunschwig, 'Zeno between Kition and Athens' (forthcoming), for reflections on evidence that Zeno was too fastidious to commit himself wholeheartedly to the Cynic lifestyle (above all D.L. VII 3), and for the suggestion that his enthusiasm for Cynicism was more theoretical than practical.

Was Zeno's adoption of these features of the Cynic way of life intended to promote the idea that following it constitutes a direct path – if not a short cut – to virtue? Probably that is what Diogenes Laertius means to imply. And the wholesale abolition in the *Republic* of temples, gymnasia and lawcourts suggests a complementary thesis: such civic institutions are of no assistance in acquiring virtue and may make it harder to achieve. Similarly, when the *Republic* in its opening pages declared general education 'useless', it doubtless meant 'useless for the acquisition of virtue'. Neither the prescriptions of the *Republic* nor the simplicities of Zeno's public image make much sense unless he thought virtue was within the grasp of anyone who was single-minded enough only to do all that was required to attain it.

But there is no evidence whatever that Zeno made any actual attempt to found a city of sages in the style he recommended in the book. We might accordingly ask ourselves: isn't that in itself evidence that the project of the *Republic* was utopian? or if not utopian, that Zeno's sincerity in proposing it is in doubt? These are theoretically distinct possibilities. It is one thing to put forward an idea that you don't think is literally speaking workable, and another to advance a proposal you believe to be workable all right, but one you don't really envisage *yourself* as the person to put into practice. This latter option, however, does not promise a plausible explanation of the facts of the present case. If Zeno thought participation in a community of the wise the practicable way anyone serious about happiness and virtue should go about acquiring them, why didn't he of all preachers obey his own teaching?

My guess is that Zeno thought that in a sense the informal community of teachers and students he presided over – or was soon to preside over[7] – in the Painted Stoa *did* itself constitute an attempt at forming a 'city of virtue'. After all, the life of reason and virtue was the goal Stoics proposed for themselves. And recall that the god Eros was the patron deity of Zeno's ideal city, and that his divine influence was to be manifested above all in the wise man's pursuit of beautiful young persons who displayed a good disposi-

[7] There is no evidence about the relative chronology of Zeno's publication of the *Republic* and his successfully gathering around him a circle more or less persuaded by his philosophical teaching. It is likely that he was already an independent teacher by the time the *Republic* appeared, but that is a different matter.

tion for virtue – with a view to developing that disposition into virtue itself. Zeno's philosophy of education seems ideally practised within a community devoted to love and friendship, conceived in the Socratic and Platonic terms analysed earlier in this book (see Chapter 2).[8] In the *Republic*'s proposals about love and friendship we are entitled to see a sort of projection of Zeno's beliefs and hopes about the life he and his associates and pupils were or would be trying to practise.[9]

On this view the *Republic* might be interpreted as at once literally and metaphorically intended. Zeno really did think the form of society he recommended in the book was practicable, and its key prescriptions about love, friendship and a life devoted to the pursuit of virtue and wisdom were ones he was attempting to live out with his pupils and associates. On the other hand the *Republic* is a contribution to a particular literary genre. Previous writers such as Plato and Xenophon[10] had effectively established the ground the author of a *Republic* might be expected by its readers to cover. Presumably much of the point of Zeno's work will have lain in its intertextuality, and in its implicit acceptance or criticism of the moral and political assumptions of his predecessors in the genre. So when he advocates not merely that women be held in common (as Plato had done) but that all the ordinary institutions of the city be dispensed with, he is above all stressing against Plato the moral indifference of all political structures of whatever kind: nothing matters in the end but virtue. Provided we take that point, it is not so important whether we actually set up communities in which the nuclear family is indeed abolished.

But Zeno's *Republic* is in no sense practicable unless virtue is

[8] Christopher Rowe points out that the very description of the god Love as a 'helper' (συνεργός) in preserving the city echoes Socrates' thesis (*Symp.* 212 B) that 'human nature can find no better helper for acquiring this [sc. virtue] than love' (see his 'The Politeiai of Zeno and Plato' (forthcoming)). For more on Zeno's deity see G. Boys-Stones, 'Eros in government: Zeno and the virtuous city', *CQ* 48 (1998) 168–74.

[9] Their intense preoccupation with erotic love is documented above (p. 28). We may assume that they shared Zeno's lofty conception of its educational purpose. The honours bestowed on Zeno by the city of Athens (D.L. VII 6) suggest that his influence on young people was generally well regarded.

[10] On Xenophon's *Constitution of the Spartans* as a model for Zeno's *Republic* see Part II of my 'Zeno of Citium's anti-utopianism' (*Saving the City*, Ch. 3).

achievable. What, then, are we to make of the Stoics' alleged acknowledgement that good men and women are in reality rarer than the phoenix ((2) above) so far as Zeno's intentions in the *Republic* are concerned? In a way there is no problem: the Stoics always held the robust view that – as is indicated by the fact that it is something people acquire – virtue is teachable (D.L. VII 91: Cleanthes, Chrysippus, Posidonius and Hecato are all cited for this view).[11] Yet there is no doubting that by the time of Cicero, at any rate, the Stoics were regarded as at least reticent in volunteering names of persons who fit their model of a sage; and their opponents felt able to use the premiss that nobody is wise without fear of being contradicted by them.[12] (When and why the colourful remark about the phoenix originated is not clear.)

Circumstantial evidence suggests that it was originally Epicurus who made the running on the general issue. He advanced the remarkable claim that nobody had ever been a wise person except for himself and his pupils (Plu. *Non posse* 1100 A; cf. Cic. *Fin.* II 70). He and the other teachers or 'leaders' (καθηγεμόνες)[13] of the Garden (Metrodorus, Hermarchus and Polyaenus – the pupils he will chiefly have had in mind) were revered by subsequent generations in the school to a degree not approached by the Stoa's respect for Zeno.[14] It therefore looks significant that Chrysippus, the first Stoic for whom an opinion on the topic is explicitly re-

[11] That it is διδακτόν is said to be clear from the fact that people change from bad to good. Posidonius took the fact that Socrates, Diogenes and Antisthenes made progress towards it as evidence that virtue is a reality (*ibid.*).

[12] See Cic. *Acad.* II 145, *ND* III 79, where Cotta seems to be brushing aside a suggestion (presumably Stoic) that their position works provided somebody *might* fit the model even if nobody actually does. Closest to Sextus' formulation is *TD* II 51, where Cicero says that *we* have never yet seen anyone possessed of perfect wisdom (although he does not there attribute this admission to the Stoics). I owe my awareness of the full range of the textual material on the topic to René Brouwer, who is devoting a chapter of his Cambridge PhD dissertation to exploring it.

[13] On καθηγεμόνες see F. Longo Auricchio, 'La scuola di Epicuro', *Cron. Erc.* 8 (1978) 21–37.

[14] Veneration of Epicurus as a god began among his own immediate pupils: Plu. *Col.* 1117 BC; Epicurus provided in his will for the continued celebration of his own birthday and those of the καθηγεμόνες: D.L. X 18–20 (for discussions of these and other relevant texts see D. Clay, 'The cults of Epicurus', *Cron. Erc.* 16 (1986) 11–28). Cf. also B. Frischer, *The Sculpted Word* (Berkeley/Los Angeles/London 1982).

corded, is described as declaring that neither he nor any of his acquaintances nor any of his 'leaders' was virtuous (Plu. *Stoic. rep.* 1048 E).[15] This sounds like an anti-Epicurean remark. It echoes Epicurean vocabulary; and it is concerned not with the general issue of who is wise or good, but with the specific and analogous problem of whether any Stoic is or was virtuous. Chrysippus seems to wish to advertise Stoic modesty in the face of Epicurean aggrandisement.[16]

Once Epicurus proposed himself a sage, it might have been expected that the Stoics would have considered whether they wished to make similar claims on their own behalf. But we may guess that they would not have lingered over the question for long. Stoics were Socratics;[17] and Socrates was celebrated for his conviction that he was not wise, but only a φιλόσοφος, lover of wisdom (cf. Plato *Symp.* 204 AB, *Phdr.* 278 D).[18] No Stoic could have thought to pretend to greater understanding than Socrates.[19] So from fairly early on in the history of the two schools the Stoics – *if they addressed the issue* – were destined to end up once again on the opposite side of the fence from the Epicureans. On the other hand, whether out of embarrassment or for whatever reason, it does not look as though they made addressing the issue one of the topics they would standardly expect to discuss in their writings or

[15] Cf. Diogenianus apud Euseb. *praep. ev.* VI 8.13: 'How do you [Chrysippus] say that only one or two people have become wise?'.

[16] This evidently remained the Stoic posture. Quintilian says the Stoics would say of Zeno, Cleanthes and Chrysippus that they were *magnos quidem . . . ac venerabiles, non tamen id quod natura hominis summum habet consecutos* (*Inst.* XII 1.18).

[17] See above all A.A. Long, 'Socrates in Hellenistic philosophy', *CQ* 38 (1988) 150–71.

[18] Although as David Sedley points out to me, Socrates *does* claim to be an expert in just one thing: matters of ἔρως (*Symp.* 177 DE; cf. *Lys.* 204 C, 206 A) – i.e. precisely Zeno's central preoccupation in the *Republic*. So it is not clear that modesty over making claims to virtue or wisdom in general would have deterred the Stoics from a sanguine view of the possibilities of practising love and friendship as Zeno had enjoined in the *Republic*.

[19] René Brouwer may be right in seeing the echo of Socrates' confession of puzzlement as to whether he is a beast more complex than Typhon or a tamer and simpler creature (*Phdr.* 230 A) attributed to Cleanthes at Sextus *M* VII 433 as reflecting Cleanthes' own appropriation of a form of Socratic doubt. The *Phaedrus* passage evidently loomed large in the problematic of Hellenistic epistemology: see Sextus *M* VII 264.

with their pupils. The sources are extremely quiet on the matter so far as concerns the Hellenistic Stoa.[20]

Perhaps the previous paragraph indulges in *a priori* history. But for the problem that concerns us – the interpretation of Zeno's *Republic* – all that matters in the end is to determine so far as we can just *when* the Stoics started to take a negative or cautious or reticent stance when asked if they could identify any actual sages.

There is some admittedly uncertain and indirect evidence for thinking that this or something like it was seen as the Stoic position in or soon after Zeno's own lifetime. Consider Sextus Empiricus' report of Zeno's argument from the reasonableness of honouring the gods to the conclusion that they exist (*M* IX 133). It was quite likely the contemporary dialectician Alexinus who propounded a counter-syllogism about the wise person also reported by Sextus.[21] From the parallel premiss that it is reasonable to honour the wise, Alexinus – if he is the critic – drew the parallel conclusion that wise persons exist. This 'did not please the Stoa', according to Sextus, 'since their wise person has to this day proved impossible to discover'. Alexinus' argument would clearly have been more pointed if it was the Stoics of his own time who were taking the line that it is at least very difficult to think of anyone who has ever attained to wisdom. The comic poet Baton (contemporary with Arcesilaus and Cleanthes)[22] may provide a further scrap of evidence. He satirises philosophers[23] in a way which suggests that outside of Epicurus' garden[24] the elusiveness of the truly good man was regarded as a philosophical commonplace (Athenaeus III 103 D, quoting from the *Fellow-Cheater*):

[20] Sextus *M* VII 432–5 makes some claims about the ignorance of Zeno, Cleanthes and Chrysippus in a context concerned with the impossibility of finding any sages, but their status as evidence is obscure.

[21] See my argument in 'The syllogisms of Zeno of Citium', *Phronesis* 28 (1983) 31–58, at pp. 34–41.

[22] See Plu. *Adul.* 55 C.

[23] Not specifically the Stoics, as Decleva Caizzi suggests (*Images and Ideologies*, p. 322). Raised eyebrows or furrowed foreheads were introduced by comic writers as a standard mark of philosophers' haughtiness, specifically Plato's in the case of Amphis Fr. 13 K. Nor is any of the other philosophical jargon Baton deploys specifically Stoic.

[24] Epicurus is mentioned a few lines earlier, in a way which suggests he is a confessed libertine, unlike the hypocrites attacked in the quoted passage.

> At any rate, take those with raised eyebrows who in their peripatetic walks and their conversations search for the wise person like a runaway slave.[25] When a little greyfish[26] is put in front of them, they know what place/topic to attack first and they search for the head/capital point as if it were a question before them – leaving everyone amazed.

But what sort of elusiveness Baton has in mind is itself elusive. Is it that non-Epicurean philosophers acknowledge that, though they can give an account of what it is to be virtuous and wise, finding anyone who has lived up to the ideal is something of a wild goose chase?[27] Or is it (perhaps more probably) that non-Epicurean philosophy is a matter of apparently interminable and inconclusive enquiry into wisdom and virtue?[28]

Let us suppose that it *was* in the time of Zeno that the Stoics began to acknowledge, under pressure from Epicurus' claim to have attained wisdom, that *they* could not identify any such person. If this happened before Zeno wrote his *Republic*, then there would be something to be said for the proposition that (3′) he thought of his good city as an unattainable – or at any rate barely attainable – ideal. For acknowledgement by those in his philosophical circle that good men are and always have been exceedingly rare birds ((2) above) could not have failed to affect the spirit in which the work was conceived. Yet it is unclear how hard this point can be pressed. As we have noted, the Stoics always stoutly maintained that virtue *does* get taught and acquired; and Zeno and his circle perhaps thought of themselves as – like Socrates – expert in matters of love and friendship in particular.

But in any case nothing in the surviving evidence prevents us from postulating the following chronological sequence:

25 Cf. also Athenaeus IV 163 B, where Baton repeats this sentence – more or less – in his *Murderer.*

26 On the greyfish, an 'unidentified' but highly prized delicacy, see J. Davidson, *Courtesans and Fishcakes* (London 1997) 6–8.

27 So Decleva Caizzi, *ibid.*

28 This interpretation is supported by Athenaeus' immediately preceding quotation, from the third-century poet Damoxenus, in which Stoics – always seeking the good, but not knowing what it is – are explicitly contrasted with Epicurus, who is the only one who does know (III 103 B).

(i) Zeno writes his *Republic*, much influenced by Cynic thinkers who assume without question that virtue is attainable if only we direct ourselves aright and put in the appropriate exertion (πόνος); Zeno's polemic against Plato at the start of his book betrays the same assumption.

(ii) Epicurus, not content with asserting (unlike philosophers of any other school) that the good is easily attainable (Phld. *Soph.* 4.12–13) and that Epicureans can live like gods among men (D.L. X 135), at some point makes the further claim that he and his principal pupils have achieved wisdom – but nobody else has (Plu. *Non posse* 1100 A).

(iii) Since Epicurus' claim raises as an explicit question: 'Have there been any truly wise or virtuous people?', the Stoics are forced to give their own response to it: 'Never – or hardly ever; and we Stoic teachers are not among the few'. Probably it is reflection upon their Socratic inheritance which moves them to respond in this way.

(iv) Alexinus formulates his counter-syllogism to Zeno's proof of the existence of gods in the light of the Stoic position articulated in (iii).

Now our supposition is that stages (iii) and (iv) as well as (i) and (ii) took place during Zeno's lifetime, although whether Zeno himself would have been party to the Stoic response postulated in (iii) one could leave open (if he was, it is surprising that no trace of the fact has survived). In any event, the important point is that stage (iii) postdates stage (i). We need not accept that when Zeno composed the *Republic* the problem of whether there had ever been any sages was perceived as a problem, still less that if he subsequently came to share the negative or agnostic answers to it proposed e.g. by Chrysippus, he would still have conceived the point of the *Republic* as being the same as when he first wrote it.[29]

[29] In his review of the first edition of this book, André Laks suggested that in differentiating Chrysippus' conception of the city (as 'proto-"jusnaturalism"') from Zeno's (as a 'proto-"republican" paradigm'), I have to 'play down the fact that Chrysippus clearly endorsed Zeno's *Politeia*' (*Ancient Philosophy* 14 (1994) 452–60, at p. 454). I am inclined to reply that Chrysippus' endorsement was perhaps a different thing from Zeno's original manifesto: while Zeno's injunction to live in a community which abandoned convention and simply practised

So the syllogism on which Philodemus' critics of Stoicism and their modern followers rely in categorising or castigating Zeno's *Republic* as utopian does not capture his intentions in writing it. He would not have subscribed to the crucial premiss (2) – that truly good persons are virtually impossible to find[30] – at the time he composed it, or conceivably at any time of his life. Even if he had, it is not clear that this would have made him think of the project of the *Republic* as merely utopian. Whether the book's proposals *were* 'impossible hypotheses for people who don't exist' is another matter. To settle that we would need to return to questions about the potentialities of human nature and the like, and engage with the bleaker assessment characteristic of those who think Realpolitik is the only way to bring order to society or to the mutual dealings of nation states.[31]

virtue was conceived as a practicable ideal, it may be that for Chrysippus – assuming he would have subscribed to premiss (2) above – Zeno's Spartan republic *had* become a utopian fantasy, valid solely for its challenge to our grasp of what is morally important and what is only indifferent from the point of view of virtue and happiness. This might explain his willingness to develop the Cynic prescriptions of Zeno's book in more extreme and sometimes more shocking directions (see p. 26 n. 10 above): one might advocate masturbation in public and incest the more outspokenly the less one really intended to engage in them.

30 The famous anecdote about his conversion to philosophy (D.L. VII 2–3) suggests that he might have reckoned at least Socrates and Crates as such.

31 My approach to the topic of this epilogue has a good deal in common with that adopted in R. Hirzel, *Untersuchungen zu Ciceros philosophischen Schriften* II 1 (Leipzig 1882) 271–98. I am grateful to the participants in the conference on Zeno and his Legacy held in Larnaca, Cyprus, in September 1998 for their comments on my first draft, and particularly to Jacques Brunschwig, Tony Long, Christopher Rowe, David Sedley and Richard Sorabji.

Bibliography

This bibliography simply lists for the reader's convenience all works cited in the notes. It is not conceived as a comprehensive or even selective guide to reading in Stoic political thought.

Editions

Pseudo-Andronicus de Rhodes 'ΠΕΡΙ ΠΑΘΩΝ', ed. A. Glibert-Thirry, Leiden, 1977.

Studi Cercidei, ed. with commentary by E. Livrea, Bonn, 1986.

M. Tulli Ciceronis De Natura Deorum, ed. J.B. Mayor, 3 vols., Cambridge, 1880–5.

M. Tulli Ciceronis De Natura Deorum, ed. A.S. Pease, 2 vols., Cambridge MA, 1958.

Clementis Alexandrini Opera, ed. W. Dindorf, 4 vols., Oxford, 1869.

Diogenes Laertius, ed. H.S. Long for the Oxford Classical Texts, 2 vols., Oxford, 1964.

Diogene Laerzio, trans. M. Gigante, Rome/Bari, 1987 (second edition).

A Hellenistic Anthology, ed. N. Hopkinson, Cambridge, 1988.

The Hellenistic Philosophers, trans. and ed. A.A. Long and D.N. Sedley, 2 vols., Cambridge, 1987.

The Art and Thought of Heraclitus, trans. and comm. by C.H. Kahn, Cambridge, 1979.

Heraclitus: The Cosmic Fragments, ed. G.S. Kirk, Cambridge, 1954.

'Towards a New Edition of Philodemus' Treatise *On Piety*', by A. Henrichs, *Greek, Roman and Byzantine Studies* 13 (1972) 67–98.

'Die Kritik der stoïschen Theologie im P. Herc. 1428', by A. Henrichs, *Cronache Ercolanesi* 4 (1974) 5–32.

Philodemus, *On the Stoics*, edited by W. Crönert in *Kolotes und Menedemos*, Munich, 1906.

'Filodemo, Gli Stoici (P. Herc. 155 e 339)', ed. T. Dorandi, *Cronache Ercolanesi* 12 (1982) 91–133.

Plato's Statesman, trans. J.B. Skemp, London, 1952.

Plutarch, *de Stoicorum repugnantiis* and *de communibus notitiis*, trans. H. Cherniss for the Loeb Classical Library in *Moralia* XIII, 2 vols., London/Cambridge MA, 1976.

Posidonius, ed. L. Edelstein and I.G. Kidd, 2 vols., Cambridge, 1972–88.

The Presocratic Philosophers, trans. and ed. G.S. Kirk, J.E. Raven, M. Schofield, Cambridge, 1983 (second edition).

Socraticorum Reliquiae, ed. G. Giannantoni, 4 vols., Naples, 1983–5.

Die Staatsverträge des Altertums vol. III, ed. H. Schmitt, Munich, 1969.

Ioannis Stobaei Anthologii: Books I and II ed. C. Wachsmuth, Berlin, 1884; Books 3 and 4 ed. O. Hense, Berlin, 1894–1909.

The Fragments of Zeno and Cleanthes, ed. A.C. Pearson, Cambridge, 1891.

Secondary literature

von Arnim, H. *Leben und Werke des Dio von Prusa*, Berlin, 1898.

Babut, D. 'Les Stoïciens et l'amour', *Revue des Etudes Grecques* 76 (1963) 55–63.

Plutarque et le Stoïcisme, Paris, 1969.

Baldry, H.C. 'Zeno's Ideal State', *Journal of Hellenic Studies* 79 (1959) 3–15.

Barnes, J. 'The Beliefs of a Pyrrhonist', *Proceedings of the Cambridge Philological Society* 208 (1982) 1–30.

Barns, J. 'A New Gnomologium: with some remarks on Gnomic Anthologies, II', *Classical Quarterly* 1 (1951) 1–19.

Belin de Ballu, E. *Olbia: cité antique du littoral nord de la mer noire*, Leiden, 1972.

Bonhöffer, A. *Die Ethik des stoikers Epictet*, Stuttgart, 1894.

Bradford A.S. 'Gynaikokratoumenoi: did Spartan women rule Spartan men?', *Ancient World* 14 (1986) 13ff.

Brunschwig, J. 'Proof Defined' in M. Schofield, M. Burnyeat, J. Barnes (eds.), *Doubt and Dogmatism*, Oxford, 1980.

Brunt, P.A. 'From Epictetus to Arrian', *Athenaeum* 55 (1977) 19–48.

Buffière, F. *Eros adolescent*, Paris, 1980.

Cartledge, P.A. 'The politics of Spartan pederasty', *Proceedings of the Cambridge Philological Society* 207 (1981) 17–36.

'Spartan wives: liberation or licence?', *Classical Quarterly* 31 (1981) 34–105.

Cavallo, G. *Libri scritture scribi a Ercolano*, suppl. I to *Cronache Ercolanesi* 13 (1983).

Cavini, W. *et al.*, *Studi su papiri greci di logica e medicina*, Florence, 1985.

Cobet, C.G. 'Zenonis Locus Emendatus', *Mnemosyne* 6 (1857) 339–40.
'Ad Clementem Alexandrinum', *Mnemosyne* 11 (1862) 334–6, 383–93.
Dal Pra, M. *Lo Scetticismo Greco*, Rome-Bari, 1975 (second edition).
Deichgräber, K. 'Polemon (9)', *RE* XXI. 2 (1952), 1288–1320.
Desideri, P. *Dione di Prusa*, Messina/Firenze, 1978.
Devereux, G. 'Greek pseudo-homosexuality and the "Greek miracle"', *Symbolae Osloenses* 42 (1967) 69–92.
Diels, H. 'Stichometrisches', *Hermes* 17 (1882) 377–84.
'Aus dem Leben des Cynikers Diogenes', *Archiv für Geschichte der Philosophie* 7 (1894) 313–16.
Donzelli, G.B. 'Un' ideologia "contestataria" del secolo IV A.C.', *Studi Italiani di Filologia Classica* 42 (1970) 225–51.
Dover, K.J. *Greek Homosexuality*, London, 1978.
'Greek Homosexuality and Initiation', in *The Greeks and their Legacy*, Oxford, 1988.
Dragona-Monachou, M. *The Stoic Arguments for the Existence and Providence of the Gods*, Athens, 1976.
Erskine, A. *The Hellenistic Stoa*, London, 1990.
Étienne, R. and Piérart, M. 'Un décret du koinon des Hellènes à Platées en l'honneur de Glaucon, fils d'Étéoclès, d'Athènes', *Bulletin de Correspondence Hellénique* 99 (1975) 51–75.
Finley, M.I. 'Utopianism Ancient and Modern', in *The Use and Abuse of History*, London, 1975.
Fortenbaugh, W.W. *On Stoic and Peripatetic Ethics: The Work of Arius Didymus*, New Brunswick/London, 1983.
Fraisse, J.-C. *Philia. La Notion d'amitié dans la philosophie antique*, Paris, 1974.
von Fritz, K. *Quellenuntersuchungen zu Leben und Philosophie des Diogenes von Sinope*, Leipzig, 1926.
Garland, R. *The Greek Way of Life*, London, 1990.
Giannantoni, G. 'Cinici et stoici su Alessandro Magno', in G. Casertano (ed.), *I filosofi e il potere nella società e nella cultura antiche*, Naples, 1988.
Giusta, M. *I dossografi di etica*, 2 vols., Turin, 1964–7.
Glucker, J. *Antiochus and the Late Academy*, Göttingen, 1978.
Goulet-Cazé, M.-O. 'Un syllogisme Stoïcien sur la loi dans la doxographie de Diogène le Cynique', *Rheinisches Museum* 125 (1982) 214–40.
L'Ascèse Cynique, Paris, 1986 (with review by J. Mansfeld, *Classical Review* 38 (1988) 162–3).

Gruen, E. *The Hellenistic World and the Coming of Rome*, vol. I, Berkeley and Los Angeles, 1984.
Hahm, D.E. 'The Diairetic Method and the Purpose of Arius' Doxography', in Fortenbaugh, *On Stoic and Peripatetic Ethics.*
Hamilton, J.R. *Plutarch: Alexander*, A Commentary, Oxford, 1969.
Hodkinson, S. 'Inheritance, Marriage and Demography: Perspectives upon the Success and Decline of Classical Sparta', in *Classical Sparta: Techniques behind her Success*, ed. A. Powell, London, 1989.
Hoïstad, R. *Cynic Hero and Cynic King*, Lund, 1948.
Inwood, B. *Ethics and Human Action in Early Stoicism*, Oxford, 1985.
Ioppolo, A.M. *Aristone di Chio e lo stoicismo antico*, Rome, 1980.
Joly, R. *Le Thème Philosophique des Genres de Vie dans l'Antiquité Classique*, Brussels, 1956.
Jones, C.P. *The Roman World of Dio Chrysostom*, Cambridge MA/ London, 1978.
Kleywegt, A.J. *Ciceros Arbeitsweise im zweiten und dritten Buch der Schrift De Natura Deorum*, Groningen, 1961.
Lammermann, K. *Von der attischen Urbanität und ihrer Auswirkung in der Sprache*, Göttingen, 1935.
Long, A.A. 'Heraclitus and Stoicism', ΦΙΛΟΣΟΦΙΑ 5–6 (1975–6) 133–56.
Maass, E. *De Biographis Graecis Quaestiones Selectae*, Berlin, 1880.
Mansfeld, J. *The Pseudo-Hippocratic Tract ΠΕΡΙ ΕΒΔΟΜΑΔΩΝ Ch. 1–11 and Greek Philosophy*, Assen, 1971.
'*Techne*: A New Fragment of Chrysippus', *Greek, Roman and Byzantine Studies* 24 (1983) 57–65.
'Diogenes Laertius on Stoic Philosophy', *Elenchos* 7 (1986) 297–382.
Marrou, H.-I. *Histoire de l'Education dans l'Antiquité*, Paris, 1965 (sixth edition).
Merlan, P. 'Alexander the Great or Antiphon the Sophist?', *Classical Philology* 45 (1950) 161–6.
Meyer, J. *Diogenes Laertius and his Hellenistic Background*, Wiesbaden, 1978.
Miller, F.D. 'Aristotle's Political Naturalism', in T. Penner and R. Kraut (eds.), *Nature, Knowledge and Virtue*: Essays in memory of Joan Kung, Edmonton, 1989.
Moles, J.L. 'The career and conversion of Dio Chrysostom', *Journal of Hellenic Studies* 98 (1978) 79–100.
Moraux, P. *Der Aristotelismus bei den Griechen*, vol. I, Berlin, 1973.
Ohly, K. *Stichometrische Untersuchungen*, Leipzig, 1928.
Powell, A. *Athens and Sparta*, London, 1988.

Rawson, E. *The Spartan Tradition in European Thought*, Oxford, 1969.

Ribbeck, O. *Agroikos*, Abhandlungen der phil.-hist. Klasse der Königlen Sächsischen Gesellshaft der Wissenschaften 10 (1888).

de Romilly, J. 'Vocabulaire et propagande, ou les premiers emplois du mot ὁμόνοια', in *Mélanges de Linguistique et de Philologie Grecques offerts à Pierre Chantraine*, Paris, 1972.

Roochnik, D.L. 'The Riddle of the *Cleitophon*', *Ancient Philosophy* 4 (1984) 132–45.

Runia D.T. *Philo of Alexandria and the Timaeus of Plato*, Leiden, 1986.

Rutherford, R.B. *The Meditations of Marcus Aurelius: A Study*, Oxford, 1989.

Schofield, M. 'The syllogisms of Zeno of Citium, *Phronesis* 28 (1983) 31–58.

'Ariston of Chios and the unity of virtue', *Ancient Philosophy* 4 (1984) 83–96.

'Ideology and Philosophy in Aristotle's Theory of Slavery', in G. Patzig (ed.), *Aristoteles "Politik"*, Göttingen, 1990.

Sedley, D.N. 'Philosophical Allegiance in the Greco-Roman World', in M. Griffin and J. Barnes (eds.), *Philosophia Togata*, Oxford, 1989.

Slings, S.R. *A Commentary on the Platonic Clitophon*, Amsterdam, 1981.

Stanton, G.R. 'The cosmopolitan ideas of Epictetus and Marcus Aurelius', *Phronesis* 13 (1968) 183–95.

Tarn, W.W. 'Alexander, Cynics and Stoics', *American Journal of Philology* 60 (1939) 41–70.

Alexander the Great, 2 vols., Cambridge, 1948.

Thesleff, H. *Studies in Platonic Chronology*, Helsinki, 1982.

Throm, H. *Die Thesis*, Paderborn, 1932.

Tigerstedt, E.N. *The Legend of Sparta in Classical Antiquity*, vol. II, Uppsala, 1974.

Trapp, M.B. 'Plato's *Phaedrus* in Second-Century Greek Literature', in D.A. Russell (ed.), *Antonine Literature*, Oxford, 1990.

Voelke, A.-J. *Les Rapports avec autrui dans la philosophie grecque*, Paris, 1961.

Wachsmuth, C. *Commentationes de Zenone Citiensi et Cleanthe Assio*, Göttingen, 1874.

'Stichometrisches und Bibliothekarisches' *Rheinisches Museum* 34 (1879) 38–51.

Walbank, F.W. 'Monarchies and monarchic ideas' in *The Cambridge Ancient History*, second edition, vol. VII.1, Cambridge, 1984.

West, M.L. 'The Orphics of Olbia', *Zeitschrift für Papyrologie und Epigraphik* 45 (1982) 17–29.

West, W.C. 'Hellenic Homonoia and the New Decree from Plataea', *Greek, Roman and Byzantine Studies* 18 (1977) 307–19.

Westman, R. 'Chrysipp III 761 und der Dialog Kleitophon', *Eranos* 59 (1961) 89–100.

von Wilamowitz-Moellendorff, U. *Epistula ad Maass*, Berlin, 1880.

Antigonos von Karystos, Berlin, 1881.

Index of passages

References in **bold** *type indicate passages translated into English.*

Index and glossary of Greek terms

General index

General index

GOLDEN AGE

MANKIND IN ITS EARLIEST DAYS LIVED IN HAPPY SIMPLICITY, SPONTANEOUSLY OBEYING THE LAWS OF DIVINE REASON.

THE ONLY PRIMITIVE INSTINCT IS SELF-CONSERVATION, WHICH ENTAILS ACTIVE BENEVOLENCE TOWARDS OTHERS. HE NEEDS OTHERS TO CARE FOR. THERE WAS AMONG THEM IGNORANCE OF VICE RATHER THAN KNOWLEDGE OF VIRTUE.

THE STATE IS THE SOLE CHECK TO MAN'S DESCENT TO CHAOS, A VERY IMPERFECT ONE COMPARED TO THE ORIGINAL COMMUNITY.

Lightning Source UK Ltd.
Milton Keynes UK
23 June 2010

155986UK00002B/2/P